Roxbury, Mass., First Universalist Soc. of Roxbury

The Semi-Centennial Memorial of the Universalist Church

Roxbury, Mass.

Roxbury, Mass., First Universalist Soc. of Roxbury

The Semi-Centennial Memorial of the Universalist Church
Roxbury, Mass.

ISBN/EAN: 9783337264185

Printed in Europe, USA, Canada, Australia, Japan

Cover: Foto ©Lupo / pixelio.de

More available books at **www.hansebooks.com**

SEMI-CENTENNIAL

MEMORIAL

OF THE

UNIVERSALIST CHURCH,

ROXBURY, MASS.

BOSTON:
UNIVERSALIST PUBLISHING HOUSE,
37 CORNHILL.
1871.

PREFACE.

The words spoken at our Semi-Centennial Anniversary afforded great satisfaction to the members of the Parish and their friends. We preserve them in this little volume, for our own sake, and that we may hand them down to those who shall keep the Centennial Jubilee.

1821.   1871.

ORDER OF SERVICES,

AT THE

SEMI-CENTENNIAL ANNIVERSARY

OF THE

UNIVERSALIST CHURCH,

ROXBURY, MASS.,

JANUARY 4, 1871.

I. ANTHEM.

II. PRAYER.
REV. ASHER MOORE.

III. SCRIPTURES.
REV. W. H. RYDER, D. D.

IV. HYMN.

V. HISTORICAL ADDRESS.
REV. A. J. PATTERSON.

VI. HYMN,—Original.
BY MRS. JANE L. PATTERSON.

VII. POEM.
REV. C. H. FAY.

VIII. HYMN.

IX. PRAYER AND BENEDICTION.
REV. J. G. BARTHOLOMEW, D. D.

COLLATION.

EVENING.

I. ANTHEM.

II. PRAYER.

III. HYMN.

IV. ADDRESSES.

V. HYMN.
BY REV. J. G. ADAMS.

VI. ADDRESSES.

VII. HYMN.

VIII. ADDRESSES.

IX. HYMN.

X. PRAYER AND BENEDICTION.

HISTORICAL DISCOURSE.

BY ADONIRAM J. PATTERSON, PASTOR.

ASSUMED THE PASTORATE SEPT., 1866.

THE first sermon preached in Roxbury, in the interests of Universalism, was delivered in the Town Hall, by Rev. Hosea Ballou, Nov. 29, 1818.* From that time meetings were held here at irregular intervals; but there were no stated services until the early part of the year 1820. An arrangement was then made between Rev. Hosea Ballou and Rev Paul Dean, ministers of the Universalist churches in Boston, to preach in the Town Hall of Roxbury on alternate Sunday evenings. The fame of the preachers attracted congregations. Their arguments and appeals fastened conviction. The people were not long in arriving at the conclusion that a religious society, built on broader foundations than any of the existing churches, was needed in this community.

A "Petition for Incorporation," signed by Samuel Parker, William Hannaford, W. J. Newman, Samuel S. Williams,

---

* Rev. Joseph Crehore informs me that, in 1798, Rev. Elhanan Winchester spent a few days at the home of his grandfather in Brookline, and preached, by invitation of the pastor, in the parish church.

and others, — forty-three in all, — was presented to the Legislature. This petition was granted, and "An Act to Incorporate the First Universalist Society in Roxbury" received the signature of the Governor on the 24th day of Feb., 1820.*

The first parish meeting under the Charter was held March 2d. Samuel Parker was chosen moderator, and Luther Newell, clerk. Two committees, consisting each of five persons, were chosen, the first "to draft by-laws," and the second "to select a piece of ground on which to erect a meeting-house for the society."

At an adjourned meeting, two weeks later, the committee on by-laws presented a report, which was adopted. These rules and regulations, with such modifications as have been made from time to time, are the recognized laws of the society to-day, as they have been through all the years of its history. The committee on "site for building" asked further time.

At an adjourned meeting, held March 30th, this committee reported that "a piece of ground at the lower end of Dudley St., and belonging to the Dudley Estate, could be procured for $1000." † They were instructed to purchase the same, the purchase money to be paid in sixty days.

On the 15th day of May a regular meeting was held, and it was voted to build a meeting-house, as soon as requisite

---

* The town of Roxbury was incorporated in 1630. The First Church was founded two years later, 1632. There was no other church in this part of the town until 1820. In this year two seceding congregations erected churches, the Baptists and the Universalists. Roxbury at that time had a population of 4,135. Boston contained 43,298 inhabitants. Boston became a city in 1822; Roxbury in 1846; the two were united in 1868. Population in 1870, 250,513.

† This church occupies the precise site of the mansion occupied by the Governors Dudley, and the well in the cellar is the same from which these eminent men drew water for themselves, their children, and their cattle.

funds could be obtained. A committee, consisting of William Hannaford, Edward Turner, Lewis Morse, Jacob Allen, Warren Marsh, Joseph Stratton, and Elisha Wheeler, was appointed, to devise ways and means, and also to recommend a plan of building.

One week later a plan was submitted and adopted, and the standing committee, consisting of William Hannaford, Edward Turner, and Lewis Morse, was instructed to carry it into effect.*

The work of building was at once undertaken. Forests, mines, and quarries contributed their stately trees and goodly stones. Strong hands derived unwonted energy from warm and loyal hearts. The foundations were laid. The timbers were fitly joined together. The edifice rose in goodly proportions. The air resounded with sound of hammer and saw, through the long summer days. But the people became impatient. A parish meeting was called on the 14th of September, and the committee was instructed to have the house completed as soon as possible.

On the 26th of December the work was finished. The members of the parish came together to make arrangements

---

* Three plans were presented, one by Architect Warren, one by Mr. Benjamin, and one by a builder whose name I have been unable to learn. The plan by Mr. Warren was accepted.

It is worthy of mention, as indicating the interest taken, even among the children, that an ingenious boy (Calvin Allen by name), seeing the plan of the proposed church on paper, carved in wood a perfect model of it with his pocket-knife, and preserved it for many years. I need hardly say that that boy — a venerable man now — is a member of this parish, and has been through its entire history.

One of the best evidences of the fidelity of the founders of this church is afforded by the fidelity of their sons and daughters. Nearly all the men, who were prominent in its affairs fifty years ago, are represented in it by their children now. And it is simple justice to say, that they take rank among the most faithful men and women of the parish, among the most high-minded and useful citizens of the city.

for the dedication. It was "voted that the dedicatory services take place on the 4th of January."

I have given these facts and dates for the purpose of showing you with what energy and zeal the founders of this church engaged in the great cause they had espoused. But few in number; without wealth or experience; beset with opposition on every hand; with no pastor to encourage them, and share their burdens with them; receiving such clerical assistance only as was lent them by the ministers of neighboring churches, within ten months of their first meeting as a legally constituted parish, they purchased this large and beautiful plot of ground, — worth to-day $100,000, — erected this commodious church, which may echo to the voice of praise for fifty years to come, and offered it in solemn dedication to the Lord.

A church of half the size would have answered their immediate wants. But they believed truth to be an aggressive power. They considered the interest of their neighbors and their children; and so, though they were only a little people, they provided a house of worship for a great congregation.

On the 4th of January, 1821, fifty years ago this afternoon, — for aught we know, fifty years ago this very hour, — this church, fresh, new, capacious, to its builders solemn and grand, was dedicated to the worship of the "One living and true God."

The sermon was preached by Rev. Hosea Ballou, from Mal. iii. 10: "Bring ye all the tithes into the storehouse, that there may be meat in mine house, and prove me now herewith, saith the Lord of Hosts, if I will not open the windows of heaven, and pour you out a blessing that there shall not be room enough to receive it." It was one of the ablest efforts of the great preacher, controversial, logical, keen as a Damascus blade, and yet warm, tender, overflowing with love to God, and kindness and good-will to men.

I am tempted to give you a brief paragraph from that sermon. After quoting the passages in the Mosaic Law, which relate to tithes and offerings (Deut. xiv.), he says, "It is seen by these scriptures, that tithes were a part of what God in his gracious providence had bestowed on his people; that they were an acknowledgment of the divine favor; that they were eaten in the place that God chose in which to establish his name and worship; eaten by those who offered them, together with their households, with rejoicing." He then shows that these tithes are typical of the gospel, and says, "As the tithes under the law, which were brought into the house of the Lord, and there eaten before the Lord, were the natural life of those who ate them; constituted their flesh and blood, and were the aliment of their support, so those truths and moral principles revealed in the life and teachings of our Saviour constitute the spiritual life of the soul, and are the aliment by which it is quickened, and by which it lives. As those tithes are brought into the house of the Lord, where God chose to put his name, so nothing but the living bread, the pure doctrine of eternal life, should be brought into our Christian worship, into the house of prayer that is dedicated to the worship of the living God. As those tithes were eaten in the house of the Lord, by those who offered them, and their families, we are instructed that in our Christian devotions we are to offer no principles, no doctrines, no sentiments, which we cannot feed upon ourselves, and on which our households cannot feed and be refreshed. Furthermore, as those tithes were to be eaten with rejoicing, we are reminded that no doctrine which issues in mourning and sorrow is a part of the gospel tithes which we are required to bring, or should ever defile a house dedicated to the worship of God."

It was an occasion of unspeakable joy to the congregation. They had given of their treasure in no stinted measure to erect this edifice. Those who were destitute of gold helped on the work with heart and hand. A still small voice whispered in each soul, "He hath done what he could," and they were confident of divine approval, and the cup of their peace was full to overflowing.

The pews in the church were at once appraised, and a goodly number of them sold. But after all had been disposed of that could be, and they had raised, as it seemed, the last dollar that could be raised, it was found that a heavy debt perilled the interests of the society. And here occurs one of those acts of heroic self-devotion and self-sacrifice which are so rare among men, and which should be held up forever as worthy of emulation and praise. It had been understood from the beginning that men who took stock in the church should receive an equivalent for their money in the pews of the church; but now it was found that the only way to relieve the parish from debt was for each man to pay for his pew a second time. This proposition was presented, and received united approval. By this means the finances of the church were placed in a sound condition.

Services were now held regularly on the Sabbath day, and the society took its place among the religious forces of the town.

On the 8th of May, 1821, an invitation was extended to Rev. Hosea Ballou, 2d, of Stafford, Conn., to become the pastor. This invitation was accepted, and Mr. Ballou was installed on the 26th of the following July. Rev. Paul Dean preached the installing sermon, from 2 Cor. vi. 3, 4: "Giving no offence in anything, that the ministry be not blamed, but in all things approving ourselves as the ministers of God." The sermon was appropriate to the occasion, excellent in spirit, and full of devotion. The services opened with an anthem, popular in those days, — " The Great Jehovah is our awful Theme," — sung by a large and excellent choir, and concluded with an original hymn of considerable merit, contributed for the occasion by John Howe, a member of the congregation, and sung to " Old Hundred," with great effect, by choir and congregation. Rev. Joshua Flagg, of Scituate, offered the opening prayer ; Rev. Richard Carrigue, of Attleboro', the prayer of installation ; Rev. Elias Smith, of Boston, the concluding prayer ; Rev. Hosea Ballou, of Boston, gave the charge, and Rev. Edward Turner the right hand of fellowship. Mr. Turner's address is a model. I never listened to or read a finer performance of its kind. If ever a prayer was answered, it is this, which occurs at the conclusion of the charge by Mr. Ballou : " May it please the Head of the Church, to make you a lasting blessing to the people of your charge, that many may say, in days to come, ' This is our friend, who taught us the religion of Jesus Christ, the love of our Heavenly Father, and the hope of eternal life.' And when your ministry shall be brought to a happy and peaceful conclusion, may your memory be as sweet as your labors shall have been faithful as ' a good steward of the manifold grace of God.'"

I recently expressed in your presence, brethren, my appreciation of this godly man ; but I want to say, here and now, that in my honest judgment Hosea Ballou, 2d, was one of the wisest of men, one of the profoundest of scholars, one of the sweetest and purest of souls. It was a fortunate day to this parish when he was chosen your first pastor. The congregation must have been favored of Heaven who were taught by him, who became the teacher of our entire ministry and church. My brethren here, who walked before me in his footsteps, and were more worthy to wear his mantle, will sustain me in the declaration, that for the solidity, the spirituality, the even prosperity of this parish through all these years, we are largely indebted to his eminently careful, faithful, and judicious leadership in the beginning of its history.

One of the first needs that claimed his attention, on assuming the pastoral office, was that of a regularly constituted church. He knew that a mere congregation gathered to hear a sermon was not enough. It only constituted the material out of which the holy temple should be fitly framed together; it must be gathered into a church, — the church of Christ. Accordingly he bent his energies in this direction. A church of twenty-two members was organized, and on the 4th of Jan., 1822, the first anniversary of the dedication of the meeting-house, it was publicly recognized. Edward Turner preached on the occasion a sermon worthy to be repeated to-day by the ablest preacher in Christendom. It is, in arrangement, in breadth and elevation of thought, in elegance of diction, in all respects, a remarkable sermon. As I read these sermons I said there were intellectual giants in those days. The fathers of this church were fed, not upon milk for babes, but meat for men.

I have before me, in Mr. Ballou's neat chirography, the Preamble, Declaration of Faith, and Uniting Compact, around which the church was gathered. It would be difficult, after fifty years of culture and experience, to improve them in a single line.*

Of the little company who subscribed this Uniting Compact forty-nine years ago to-day, not one remains. They held

---

* See Appendix A.

up the pastor's hands while he prayed, until the going down of the sun. But pastor and people have fulfilled the condition, and entered into the promised inheritance, "Be thou faithful unto death, and I will give thee a crown of life."

On the 15th of August, 1830, a meeting was called of those who were "especially interested in the religious training of the young." It was voted, that "the instructors of the First Universalist Sunday School organize themselves into a body, the title of which shall be, the Board of Instructors of the First Universalist Sunday School in Roxbury." A constitution was adopted, and the following officers were elected, viz.: Mrs. Dudley Williams, 1st Superintendent; Miss Sarah Turner, 2d Superintendent; George F. Cook, Secretary; John D. Young, Librarian. It may be interesting to our strong-minded sisters, to know that the first Superintendents of this very successful school were women, and that for seven years it performed an efficient service, with women at its head. Whether the growth of the school, or a change of public sentiment, with regard to the "*sphere of woman*," caused a man at length to be chosen as leader, we have been unable to determine; this we do know, that from first to last, the Sunday school has been one of our most efficient and successful departments of Christian labor.

Mr. Ballou remained here in the faithful discharge of his pastoral duties seventeen years. He was supported by a band of men and women, scarcely less able in guarding the secular and other interests of the church than he was in directing its spiritual affairs. In examining the records of the parish, church, and Sunday school, during all those years, one is constantly impressed with the dignity, taste, and propriety which characterized their deliberations. Every vote, resolution, recommendation, or report, is expressed in almost faultless language. There is scarcely a grammatical blunder, a mistake in orthography, an inelegant expression, or a blot on the record, during all those years.

Seventeen years make many changes in a parish. Within that period more than half the inhabitants of our globe pass to their eternal rest, and a new generation rise up to tread in their footsteps. A large proportion of the men and women who welcomed Mr. Ballou when he came here, had been borne to "the narrow house appointed for all the living." An unspeakable sense of loss possessed him as he witnessed their vacant places; and he came at length to the conclusion that his own peace of mind, and perhaps the interests of the church, required a change.

In his letter of resignation, bearing date April 28, 1838, he says, "The death of so many of the elder members of the society has long weighed heavily on my spirits; and recent afflictions of this kind have increased the oppression, until it has become extremely painful. When I stand in the desk to address you, I look around for the fathers of the society, but, with very few exceptions, they are not there." He also hints, that "some of his parishioners did not find his ministrations edifying, and that their taste was for a different style of performance;" which feeling, I think, had something to do with his resignation, as it does with nearly every ministerial resignation. His letter concludes with these words of brotherly love and counsel: "Brethren, I have spent the best part of my life with this society. I have been with most of its members in trouble and in joy. The younger have grown up under my eye, and are to me as sons and daughters. With most of the older, I have been an associate of equal age. If the sacred relation which I have so long sustained to them gives me a right to an earnest expression of my heartfelt desire, I would entreat that the change of pastors may not alienate a single member from the society, nor abate the zeal of any one in avowing and supporting 'the Gospel of the grace of God.'"

From April, 1838, until Jan., 1839, the parish was without a pastor. Rev. Asher Moore, of Hartford, Conn., then received and accepted an invitation to the pastoral relation. He came, bringing fine gifts as a preacher, added to the zeal of youth. Bright hopes were entertained of a long and successful ministry; but the rigor of our climate, a feeling of homesickness on the part of his family, and a call to Philadelphia, caused him to sever the connection at the end of the first year.

Rev. Cyrus H. Fay was invited to succeed him, and commenced his labors in Jan., 1841. If Br. Fay were not by my side, I would say some things about him, which I cannot utter with the same freedom in his presence, — a little praise is apt to spoil a minister, you know; but it will not do him any harm, I trust, to read what was written and printed concerning him, oh, many and many years ago. He doubtless read it with some interest, when he needed such words more, and, perhaps, thought of them more, than he does now. Said a writer concerning him, as long ago as when he was your minister, "Gifted with rare power of argument and illustration, with a ready utterance and an agreeable manner in the pulpit, and possessing those qualifications as a pastor which designate him as a man of the people and a shepherd of the flock, it is hoped that he may be long spared to a work, than which there can be none greater among men, — that of a good minister of Jesus Christ."

The settlement of Mr. Fay was followed by such an increase, that larger accommodations were required for the

Sunday school. Up to this time the sessions of the school had been held, first in a small lecture-room over the vestibule of the church, and then, as the school increased, in a hall which was hired for the purpose; but it was rapidly outgrowing these accommodations.

At a special parish meeting, called to consider its needs, on the 8th of February, 1841, a committee, consisting of Joseph Stratton, Tilson Williams, H. H. Williams, John C. Seaver, William White, and Luther Bullock, was chosen, to get a plan of a vestry, to ascertain the cost thereof, and to gain, if possible, information respecting the amount of money which could be raised by subscription in aid of its construction.

At a subsequent meeting this committee reported, " that they found part of the society in favor of building a vestry, part in favor of paying a debt due the estate of S. S. Williams, and part in favor of building sheds for the protection of their horses from the winter storms." The committee were of the opinion, " that the interests of the society would be promoted by accommodating all these parties;" and they respectfully recommended " that the debt be paid; that a vestry forty-five by thirty feet — the estimated cost of which was $1,000 — be built on the north-west corner of the land belonging to the society; and that sheds be built by such persons as desired them, at an expense of thirty dollars each, under the supervision of the Standing and Building Committees. The committee " were happy to say, that they had found a zeal in the cause surpassing their expectations," that they " had succeeded in getting the subscription up to $1,400," and no doubt " that funds could be raised to discharge the debt and erect the buildings; as there were many who, from lack of time, had not yet enjoyed the pleasure of putting their names on the subscription paper."

I submit, brethren, that this was an original and interesting way of settling differences of opinion. Some wanted to pay the debt; others were for building a vestry; others, still, wanted sheds built to protect their animals. Less resolute and consecrated men would have spent weeks in impatient disputation, and nothing would have been accomplished. Or, if the vestry was built, the expense would have been borne by a few individuals, and the rest would have hung back, grumbling because the debt was not paid, or because there was no mercy shown to the dumb animals. These men did all at a stroke,— paid the debt, built the vestry and the sheds, removed all sources of dissension, satisfied everybody, and the church was strengthened, and good feeling prevailed.

Mr. Fay's ministry covered a period of nearly nine years, during which fifty-two members were added to the church, the Sunday school and congregation were enlarged, and harmony and good feeling prevailed.

His letter of resignation bears date March 26, 1849. It expresses the kindest feelings toward the society and all its members, young and old. The only reason assigned for severing the pastoral relation was failing health. He hoped that needed rest would be secured with change. In a series of resolutions, the society reciprocated his kindly feeling, saying, among other good things, that "By his fidelity to the cause of truth, the wants of humanity, and the interests of education, he had endeared himself to the members of the society and the entire community."

The sorrow felt at Mr. Fay's removal found its solace in the settlement of Rev. W. H. Ryder, the following November. He entered the field bringing with him a rare combination of ministerial qualities. To the zeal and fervor of youth he added a well-balanced and well-disciplined mind, sound common sense and discretion, dignity of character and manners quite beyond his years, accurate and impressive elocution, a genial disposition, that warms and wins, and an entire consecration to the work of the ministry. He came with his mind and heart rested, refreshed, intensified, by travels in Europe and the Holy Land ; glad to be at home again, and longing to resume the duties of his profession. He was in the very best condition of body and mind, to make a successful beginning in a new field of labor. He did not go about his work as a duty, but he engaged in it with exquisite pleasure. He enjoyed intensely, — partly from constitutional fitness, and partly from the elastic condition he was in, — what seems to other men, and under other circumstances, the drudgery of pastoral life.

Accordingly he became the intimate friend, the familiar companion, as well as the acceptable preacher. Few ministers ever experienced a more happy, harmonious, or successful pastorate ; few ever left behind them sweeter, tenderer, or more sacred memories.

Soon after he was called, the society took measures to procure an organ. Up to that time they had depended, for an accompaniment to the voices in singing, upon an orchestra of wind and stringed instruments. But they must have now the one grand instrument which includes so many others, and which has been especially dedicated to the worship of the sanctuary, and an organ was purchased at a cost of $1,400.

Time passed on. The interest deepened. It began to be whispered that the church was a little behind the times, — not in keeping with the preaching or the congregation. It must be renovated and improved. "So the workmen wrought, and the work was perfected by them, and they strengthened the House of the Lord and repaired it." The high pulpit of the olden time was taken down. The old square pews were exchanged for the more graceful circular slips of modern times. The brush of the painter touched the soiled and uncomely walls, and gave them a fresh and inviting aspect.

The inner temple, too, was renovated, — the temple of the Holy Ghost. Souls flocked to the altar of the church, and received the sprinkling of baptismal water, and sat down with great joy around the table of a common Master. One hundred and thirty-six members were added to the church during Br. Ryder's administration. It was an era of general good feeling. Minister and people walked together, as "with one heart and one soul."

Now it was whispered through the society, that the pastor had been invited to settle in a distant city. Few believed that he would accept the invitation. Still a feeling of foreboding took possession of the people. A parish meeting was called to take some definite action, and assure the pastor in an emphatic way of the love and confidence of his parishioners.

The following preamble and resolutions were unanimously adopted : —

" *Whereas*, we have learned that our pastor, Rev. W. H. Ryder, has received an invitation to assume the pastoral charge of a society in Chicago, Ill., and that he is considering the propriety of accepting the same ; therefore,

" *Resolved*, That in view of the kindly and harmonious relations existing between us as pastor and people, and considering the best interests of our society, it is our earnest desire that the present connection be not dissolved.

" *Resolved*, That Br. Ryder be requested to remain."

Two days later, a long letter was received from the pastor.

tendering his resignation. In that letter he says: "For nearly ten years we have labored, rejoiced, sorrowed together. Nothing has transpired to mar our prosperity or alienate us from each other. There is not a man, woman, or child in the parish who has not a share in my good-will; nor to my knowledge is there one whose confidence and affection do not reach out kindly toward me. Under these circumstances I have found it exceedingly hard to adjust my sympathies to the decision of my judgment, and to accept the fact, that after a few short weeks I am to be no longer the minister of this people. I do hope and pray that I may bear your love and sympathy with me to my new field of duty, and be always — as from time to time I may return here — a welcome friend in your midst. Your hearts are large enough to hold me and mine, though we are bodily a thousand miles away, and though you give to my successor — as I hope and pray you will — the same generous support, the same Christian sympathy, and hearty co-operation that have been given to me. The Lord be with you, and keep you faithfully unto the end."

The pastor gone, a successor must be provided. To fill the place made vacant would require no ordinary man. The wise men of the parish surveyed the ministerial ranks both near and afar. At length all eyes turned in one direction. There seemed a kind of poetic justice in calling from the West its bright particular star.

And so Rev. J. G. Bartholomew — the man of "silver tongue" — was called. He brought with him a fascinating eloquence. He tripped along, through fields of thought and flowers of rhetoric, as gracefully and as freely as the gazelle trips over a prairie. He played with the hearts of men as a musician plays upon an instrument. He held you as in a spell by the charm of his speech. Now he swept the exultant keys, and your faces gleamed and your eyes lit up with the inner fire. Now he touched the minor notes, and your eyes moistened with tears. Multitudes thronged the gates of the sanctuary, and every sermon seemed a new inspiration and delight.

Then came the dark wave of *War;* and the hearts of the people were failing with sudden fear; and tears were in all your homes, and lamentations were in all your streets. The young minister rose up to meet it like a tower of strength. He exposed the crime of rebellion with a caustic eloquence which made traitors deny their disloyalty, and wavering men swing into line. He upheld the cause of perilled country with an enthusiastic power which changed common men to heroes, and prepared them to ask the privilege of dying to maintain its honor. He confirmed your faltering faith in the darkest day; and said prayers and shed tears over your slaughtered sons; and led on in the "good fight" until loyalty prevailed, and peace was restored, and the republic saved, and the manacles fell broken from the limbs of every slave.

There was little opportunity to enlarge churches, or purchase organs, or even gather souls into the church during those awful years. The call of the preacher was to keep the flame of loyalty burning; the business of the people, to provide lint and cordial for the wounded, burial for the dead, and give themselves as seed for the furrows ploughed by the share of war. The minister that did this most effectively answered best the divine call. The people who were most efficient here, responded most acceptably to the appeals of Heaven. Judged from this stand-point, where was the minister or the church, that wrote a better record than your own, that more truly earned the approbation of Heaven and the gratitude of men!

Nor were the spiritual interests of the congregation neglected. The Sunday school was never larger or in better condition; and eighteen members were added to the church during Br. Bartholomew's administration.

After a ministry of nearly six years, he tendered his resignation, to accept the pastoral charge of the Fourth Universalist Church, Brooklyn, N. Y., the resignation to take effect Jan. 1, 1866. At a parish meeting, called to take action on this resignation, it was unanimously resolved, "That the ministry of Br. Bartholomew, by its rare ability, has been eminently successful in making the church a place where old and young have delighted to assemble, and worship with devout and cheerful spirit our heavenly Father, and it is with feelings of sincere regret that we receive his letter, severing the pleasant connection which has existed between us as pastor and people."

At the annual meeting in March following, the Standing Committee, consisting of Daniel Jackson, George Warren, and Charles D. Swain, in connection with a committee of three from the Sunday school, were instructed "to consider the propriety of enlarging the vestry, procure plans and estimates, and report at an adjourned meeting." This was the initial step which resulted during the summer in putting the chapel in its present enlarged and improved form, at an expense of about $3,500.

My acquaintance with the parish began in May, and my pastoral connection in September of the same year (1866).

From personal knowledge I can testify that since that time you have been a busy people. The *special* improvement, which should be named in this epitome of our history, is the change that has been made in the form of the church, and the setting up here of this large and elegant organ.

At an adjourned annual meeting, held March 11, 1868, the standing committee, consisting of George Frost, Charles D. Swain, George Warren, Eben. Alexander, and J. A. Brigham, was instructed "to consider the subject of a new organ, in all its bearings, and report at a future meeting." The committee subsequently reported in favor "of procuring an organ, and of making such alterations in the church, and additions to it, as would provide a place for the organ in the rear of the pulpit; pastor's room, choir room, &c." To the objection that it were "better to put a new roof on the church than to make these additions to it," it was moved by one of our young men,* in the exact spirit of the fathers, to whom we referred a little while ago, "that we settle these differences of opinion, by meeting the wishes of all; that we make the needed additions to the church; that we buy a new organ; and that we also slate and make such other repairs on the church as are needed for our comfort and its preservation." The proposition was accepted in its length and breadth, and none will doubt to-day, I think, that it was timely and wise.

Not only have you carried out in this regard all that was proposed, but you have contributed liberally and on several occasions to the interests of missions and education. You have raised for various purposes, within the past five years, — in addition to current expenses, — the round sum of $20,000. You have remembered the poor, "whom ye have always with you." You have fostered the Sunday school, and shown a becoming zeal in all moral and social reforms. You have brought your children to the altar, — more than a hundred in all, — and dedicated them to the Lord. Fifty-one persons have professed faith in Christ, and been baptized

---

* Christopher Tilden.

into his church. This is a meagre report, as contrasted with our large desires; but it shows that you are not destitute of material or spiritual life.

I want to say to you, brethren, in this presence, you have done well. I want to thank you for your co-operation and consecration. I believe these children and grandchildren are wearing worthily the mantles of the fathers.

I would be glad, if I had time, to speak particularly of the men who, during the fifty years of our history, have watched over the church as though it were their family, contributing to its welfare by their wisdom, their toils, and their prayers. How they throng about us, a glorified multitude, their brows radiant with the light of heaven!

There is Parker, who, though he sat for years at the receipt of customs, surrounded by all the temptations of official station, could say with the good publican, " If I have taken aught from any man by false accusation, I restore unto him fourfold."

And there is Newman, forming character, day by day, amid the rough experiences of life, as he formed iron at his forge, strengthening the fibres of integrity and honor by manly contact with the world, as the sinews of his arm were strengthened at the anvil by repeated blows.

And there are Deacons Stratton, Watson, Marsh, and Burrill, whose godly walk and conversation caused them to be selected as the bearers of the vessels of the Lord.

And there are the Williamses, and the Morses, and Hannaford, and Mayo, and Howe, and Turner, and Myrick, and Gale, and Goddard, and Faxon, and Davenport, and the late Jesse Jordan, — patient, uncomplaining, suffering man, — last of that faithful company of corporate members to finish his work on earth and pass on to his reward.

Later we find Guild and Hersey, Hastings and Humphrey,

John C. Seaver * and Francis Dana, A. W. Newman, J. W. Parker, and other names equally worthy of honorable mention, some of whom are still with us, and some have passed from sight.

One cannot read the records of the parish without being convinced that from the beginning it has been under the direction of calm, thoughtful, discreet, and consecrated men. There are few lines upon its records which one could wish to erase. There are few motions or resolutions which are a discredit to the taste or the judgment of the minds that framed, or the votes which adopted them.

I should do injustice to my own feeling, and subject myself to the rebuke of all these ex-pastors, and the members of the congregation, if I failed to mention especially that manly man, descended through a line of governors from a lordly ancestry, who, for so many years, collected and disbursed the revenue of the society. If ever there was a faithful official, Joseph W. Dudley was that official. For the healthy condition of your finances during the past thirty years you are largely indebted to his vigilant care. The pastors, who one after another occupied this pulpit, will remember him with especial gratitude. They will never forget the peculiar way in which — meeting us in the aisle or in the vestibule, when the quarter came round — he would say, "Call at the office to-morrow, and I will take care of

---

* Mr. John C. Seaver was a young man, just finishing his apprenticeship, when the church was built. He had no money to subscribe, so he promised, as his contribution, to glaze the windows, every light of which he set with his own hands. It should also be recorded to the everlasting honor of this good man, that the first fifty dollars he ever earned, or possessed, he appropriated to the purchase of half a pew in this church. He has often said it was the best investment of his life.

Just as this work was going to press, this good man fell quietly asleep in the joyful hope of a glorious immortality.

you." It was one of the fundamental doctrines of his religion, that the minister is a man, needing food, and raiment, and shelter, just like other men; that the laborer is worthy of his hire, and that a failure to receive it at the appointed and expected time may embarrass him just as it would any other man. He would not let us feel that we were dependents. When we thanked him for a payment, as it was our pleasure to do, he would respond, "*No thanks! It's yours!* You've earned it!" often adding, "I wish it was more!" and sometimes saying, with a bright twinkle in his eye, that when he "hired a man, and paid him promptly, he expected him to stay at home and do his own work, and not be running off and sending some bungler in his place." This was his way of expressing a kindly interest in his minister, — not that he thought us better than our neighbors, or objected at all to an occasional exchange. Peace to his ashes! Blessings on his memory! He wears a crown among the sanctified!

The secretaries, too, who have recorded your doings for the past fifty years,* should receive special and honorable mention. This is one of the most difficult and laborious offices connected with the secular management of the church. To fill it acceptably requires care, taste, culture. One must be able to take a thought, in however crude a form it may be presented, and, on the instant, clothe it in appropriate language, without destroying its identity, or changing in the slightest degree its meaning.

I have examined your records from the opening to the closing paragraph, with mingled surprise and admiration. They have been kept with wonderful care. The chirography is plain and clean as a printed page. There is scarcely an

---

* See Appendix C.

inaccuracy either in grammar or orthography. Everything is preserved that is essential to a full and accurate history of the parish, and yet the pages are not lumbered with superfluous verbiage or irrelevant resolutions.

To Luther Newell, Eben Brewer, Joseph Bugbee, Geo. B. Davis, Calvin Brown, Charles Marsh, and Joseph H. Streeter, this parish owes an everlasting debt of gratitude. They have most of them passed on. The hands, once so faithful, are dust. But their works follow them.

I wish I had time to speak of them separately as their personal worth deserves; especially of young Marsh,— the gifted, cultivated, high-minded, and pure-hearted man, who brought the wealth of his mind and character, and laid it on the altar of the church, and then, when religion was beginning to hope so much from him, was translated from these earthly scenes to the rewards of paradise.

But I must pass to say a word concerning the faithful workers in the Sunday school. From the time the school was organized it has been led by an efficient and self-sacrificing corps of officers and teachers. As is usually the case, this important interest has been committed to the young men and women more than it should be. But I am happy to say, that with few exceptions our young people have fulfilled their solemn trust with a fidelity and ability which was an honor to themselves and a blessing to the school. And we have had a few men and women who were willing to devote the experiences of age to the welfare of the children. Their white locks are and have been a benediction, and I know they will testify, that in their efforts to do good in the school they have received abundant blessing. One of our teachers* entered the school when it was organ-

---

* Franklin Williams, Esq.

ized, as a member of the infant class, and has been in it, as a pupil, teacher, or officer, through all the years. After serving efficiently for many years as superintendent, he returned to his place as a teacher, saying that when he entered the school he enlisted for life. Surely his example is worthy of imitation. There are other members of the school, who have been in service nearly as long, and are entitled to equal praise. From the day it was organized the progress of the school has been steadily onward. For years it has taken rank among the largest and most efficient schools in the city. It was never in better condition than now. The good it has done can only be estimated when all influences, and all secrets are revealed in heaven.

Let me lay my closing tribute at the feet of the faithful women of the parish, who have contributed so much to all that is best in its history. From the time that Jane Cheeny signed the Petition for Incorporation, our women have been foremost in every good word and work. Their hopeful voices have given courage in the darkest days; their helpful hands have lightened the heavy load; their warm, loving hearts have watched over the church as though it were a child. Their names do not appear on the parish books as do the names of their husbands, brothers, and sons; but their mighty spirits have worked in, and through, and behind these visible wheels; and on the *church roll* their names are written, and in the "Lamb's Book of Life."

You need not be ashamed of your history. There have been no marked reverses, no serious dissensions, no dark shadows. Your course has been steady, even, upward. God has dealt tenderly with this vine. It has grown, not like Jonah's gourd, which sprang up in a night, and withered with the sunrise, but like a healthy tree, that grows for a hundred years, and bears fruit for ages.

So far as it is modest for me to speak, I will say that you have been most fortunate in your ministers. There has never been a breath of scandal on one of their names. They have all held fair rank as preachers and scholars; and some of them have taken the first position for ability, culture, and devotion to every good cause. There has been no marked failure, no great shame, — such as comes upon some churches, — thus far in your history.

If you have been fortunate in your shepherds, they have been equally happy in their flock. I have no doubt that when we are ready to seal up and lay away the book of our ministerial life, we will all find that some of its brightest pages were written in Roxbury; some of our happiest experiences were in this church and among this people.

The past is behind us, brethren, with all its lessons, encouragements, warnings. The present is around us, with its grand opportunities and solemn responsibilities. The future is before, beckoning us onward. Another fifty years will come and go, and we men and women will all be in our graves. Let us gird ourselves for our tasks, remembering that living well to-day, we enrich eternity.

HYMN,— Original.

By Mrs. Jane L. Patterson.

Our fathers saw the vision bright,
    Which came to Jacob while he slept,
And marked the dawning of the light,
    Like him, with vows inviolate kept.

"God's house" arose, a pillar fair,
    Of faith which knows no shadows dim, —
A ladder from the altar stair
    To heights of perfect bliss with Him;

And where in gracious ministry
    The angels go, and come again,
And God, above it, tenderly
    Sends down his promises to men.

Along the years we count to-day,
    What hosts these hallowed aisles have pressed,
Who here have found the shining way, —
    The very gate of heavenly rest!

For all thy gifts, O God, to us,
    A people blest beyond compare,
Our grateful hearts in sacred trust
    Would onward still, the vision bear.

POEM.

BY REV. CYRUS H. FAY.

Pastor from January, 1841, to March, 1849.

As one returns, who long abroad has strayed,
To that loved spot where he in childhood played,
There to relive awhile the life of yore,
When wavelets bright came singing to the shore,
And morning's sunshine fell in splendors warm,
Untroubled yet by whirlwind and by storm, —
So come I back, obedient to your call,
To keep with you this fitting Festival.

And, friends, forgive me if, as backward thrown,
My heart first yields to impulse all its own.
'Twas here I spent my manhood's hopeful prime,
And drank, at times, the sweetest draughts of time.
Ah, yes; and while I bore to mourning hearts relief,
To my sad lips was pressed the bitter cup of grief!
Too strong the sway of mem'ry in this hour;
I cannot choose, but yield me to her power.

By Queechy's bright, rock-ruffled sheen,
On Woodstock's fair and pleasant "Green,"

I heard your call, and hither came
To preach in my great Master's name,
And lead this flock by waters still,
Obedient to his holy will.
How dared I then such trust assume!
How hope my rush-light would illume,
Where suns had shone with steady ray!
Think of a taper making day!
But here I toiled from year to year,
Wrought on in weakness and in fear, —
Yet saw the blade in beauty grow,
And ear, and full corn's golden glow.
I only watered what was sown
By hands more skilful than my own;
And He who sent his Son to save,
The sunlight threw and increase gave.

But where's the Town I came to then?
Roxbury, most aptly named by men;
With ragged pudding-stones bestrown,
And vacant fields all brier-sown;
Rough roadsides where the barberries grew,
And lanes the lovers wandered through.
Ah, me, how smart some places are!
Mounted on progress' gilded car,
They court the great world's senseless stare,
By doffing rustic garb and air,
And aping city styles and ways;
Strutting in fashion's hoops and stays;
Yielding to pride their very names,
And all their old historic claims.
Thus Roxbury, once so widely known,
Has into Boston Highlands blown.
Well might the rocks their heads conceal,
The briers from the pastures steal,

Soured barberries from the roadsides start,
And old-time fences all depart!

Is this the church my eyes beheld
In those departed days of eld?
That church from these foundations rose,
The terror of its bigot foes;
But lone it stood, no chapel near,
Nor horse-sheds gaping in its rear.
The spire and belfry are the same;
Familiar, too, this bulky frame;
But frescoed wall, and modern pew, —
Sure these are features wholly new.
Still greater changes o'er me creep,
I've had a Rip Van Winkle sleep;
Of old, the organ rose, high-throned,
Under the bell, as solemn-toned;
A modest organ, too, it stood,
And ever in devoutest mood,
Scorning all airs aristocratic,
And strains or snatches operatic;
If heard to-day its sacred strain
Would bring the old times back again
When, fogies say, they'd less of gammon,
And God was worshipped more than mammon.
Just here, where in the days of old
The rear wall rose so bare and cold,
Another instrument appears,
To storm indiff'rence through the ears;
And, nolens volens, make devout,
By putting worldly thoughts to rout!
What power there is o'er human kind,
In cool, audacious, noisy wind!
The strange old pulpit, too, I miss,
A watch-tower high compared with this;

I have its picture in my mind;
The thing itself I nowhere find.
Grandly it rose above the floor,
As if to teach our thoughts to soar
Away from grovelling things of time,
To heights empyrean and sublime!
Two fluted columns at the base
Relieved the sameness of its face;
And back of these two doors were hung:
The one was seldom open swung,
A closet close it hid from view,
Whose secrets only deacons knew;
The other opened to the stairs,
Which upward led, where lighter airs
Around the preacher's brow did blow,
Than fanned his hearers down below.
No "*leaning* miracle" it stood,
Like that by Arno's classic flood;
But straight and square, with sternest front,
Ready for battle's fiercest brunt;
Well suited to those times gone by,
When theologic strife ran high,
And down from pulpit tops were shot
Both ball and bomb-shell hissing hot!

And here I am constrained to tell
What once in such strange desk befell:
A preacher, from another State,
Was serving as a "candidate,"
Anxious to please his hearers all,
And gain, of course, the loudest "call."
The organ's symphony was given,
Petition had been made to heaven,
The two hymns sung, the Scriptures read,
The text announced; and now the thread

Of wise discourse began to show
Its quality to minds below.
Till then, nor sight nor jarring sound
Had marred devotion's spell profound;
Even a dog was still the while,
And couchant in the central aisle;
Both head and tail were in repose;
But think not he had come to doze, —
As men are sometimes said to do, —
(Of course, no reference's made to you);
Not he; for now his nose is ruffed,
As if schismatic scent he snuffed.
(And dogs like this we still may see,
Smelling about for heresy.)
He rose; and, looking gravely where
The preacher spoke with grace and care,
He raised his tail, and shook his head,
Then up the aisle did gravely tread;
The door he passed, the stairway trod,
And reached, at length, the man of God,
Who heard his foot-fall on the stairs,
Yet gave no sign of mundane cares;
But growing fervor he displayed,
And gestures more emphatic made.
The zealot dog, as if to tease,
Against the pulpit knocked his knees,
By rubbing hard, as dogs can do,
And have done more than once to you.
But still the preacher kept his course,
Defiant of all canine force,
Hoping the while the stubborn brute,
Finding he was not made to suit
A pulpit either high or low,
Would down the dizzy stairway go.

But harder trial was to come ;
The dog began to feel at home.
Again he rubbed against his calves
With all his force, — and not by halves, —
Till shook the good man heels and head,
And almost snapped the sermon's thread !
This was repeated once, twice, thrice ;
And then the creature, in a trice,
Rose up full length, and laid his paws
Where fists had smote in virtue's cause.
One glance he took, short, sharp, intent,
Then, with a bound, he downward went,
And round the aisles as wildly ran,
As frightened mastiff only can,
Filling the church to ceiling high,
With his resounding, shrill " Ki-yi ! "
You do not wonder at his fright,
When you recall the pulpit's height.
Nor do you ask if mirthful smiles
Brightened between the vacant aisles,
Or giggles tripped in merry chase
Of those wild echoes round the place.
But did the preacher *all* defy,
And still discourse with gravity?
He did, my friends, nor was this all ;
His stern persistence won a call.
Dear hearers, did you fail to note
Two morals in my anecdote?
The first is this, — and hold it fast, —
Persistence gains its end at last,
In spite of dogs and demons too,
And all a mocking world can do.
The second moral is for those
Whose zeal for creed no caution knows ;

Mount not above your wonted plain,
Lest faint and dizzy grows the brain,
And you come tumbling back again ;
While your chagrin the worldling mocks
With smile and jeer unorthodox.

Yes, change that worketh everywhere,
Was busy in this house of prayer,
While passed the hours of light and shade,
Since first its outlines I surveyed.
The old, familiar to our view,
We miss with sadness, though the new
Was shaped 'neath skilled improvement's eyes,
And hued with beauty's matchless dyes.

But where are the *faces* that answered to mine,
With the language of love, in days of lang syne?
But few with this gladness are beaming to-day,
And the many have gone from our temple away.

As leaf follows leaf from their home on the trees,
Unloosed by the frost, and borne down by the breeze ;
So friend follows friend till the winter winds moan,
And we miss them and sigh as we linger alone.

Of those I am thinking, who languished of yore,
And passed from my view to the ever green shore ;
Their features grow bright to my fancy again,
All trustful and calm and transfigured by pain.

The aged I see, who, like Simeon old,
Were anxious to walk on those pavements of gold,
Gleaming bright in a sun whose disc never dips
'Neath a dusky horizon, nor sinks in eclipse.

And those I behold, at the noontide of life,
Who stepped from the ranks, and who ceased from the strife ;

Though wounded and bleeding, no murmur they sighed,
But, of victory sure, in tranquillity died.

The young and the beautiful, too, I recall,
Who went with a smile to the Father of all;
Exchanging the playthings and pleasures below
For the joys of that life which the seraphim know.

Say, do they remember, where blissful they dwell,
The prayers that we said and the whispered farewell,
When darkness came down, as they yielded their breath,
And strengthened my faith by their triumph in death?

Oh, could I but know that the lessons I read,
Petitions I made, or some word that I said,
Illumined the gloom of death's gathering night,
And helped them to walk through its silence in light!

Be patient, O heart, for the time draweth nigh
When we shall commune in the mansions on high;
And yearnings like thine shall have utterance meet,
While the answers of love will our raptures complete.

But earlier days now claim our view,
When upward this strong structure grew;
A protest bold against all creeds
That mocked affection's deepest needs,
And aimed devoutness to inspire
With flashes of infernal fire.
Unblest by priests with silken stoles,
Accursed by all fanatic souls,
It slowly rose from base to vane,
And stood complete the bigot's bane,
Throwing its shadow on his path,
Unsmitten by a bolt of wrath.

Ah, in those goodly times of old,
Not all that glittered was pure gold.
Stern in religion's sacred sphere,
Mad zealots stalked with eyeballs blear;
Seeing no good beneath the sun
That was not by their favor done;
Frowning on all who meekly trod
The better way that led to God;
Who human weakness seemed to see,
Without one throb of charity;
Dealing about splenetic thumps,
All their religion in the dumps.
'Tis said that in that olden day
Grave ministers could drink and pray,
And pray and drink, with each and all,
Going their round parochial;
And when the holy Sabbath came,
Would soar with fervor all aflame,
Attaining heights beyond the reach
Of those who now on water preach!
The singers, then, a tuneful band,
Kept a decanter near at hand;
And, while the parson did his part, —
Or roughly, or with knightly art
His lances threw sheer o'er the pews,
Against the vices of the Jews,
Or Gentile sins of *ancient* days, —
They wet their lips for louder praise.
If this was so, without a bribe,
Believe we, deacons did imbibe;
Took just enough their zeal to fire,
And rouse and fan their holy ire
Against dissenters "vile and bold,"
And all recusants from their fold.

Here lived a deacon, I have heard,
Whose spirit was profoundly stirred
By this transaction of your sires.
He hurled against it shafts of wit,
And oft invoked the strangest fires,
All red and glowing from the pit!
'Tis said that once this saintly soul
Had sipped the tavern's tempting bowl,
'Till sleep came o'er him at midday,
And prone upon the bench he lay;
Not drunk! oh, no! but in that state
When care knocks vainly at the gate,
And safe within from mundane foes,
Tired piety can take a doze.
In just a doze — no more, no less —
Had sunk the deacon's saintliness,
As now my narrative will show:
A teamster, hunting high and low,
Through street and lane, where team could go,
Abruptly oped the tavern door,
And, loud as bulls of Bashan roar,
Asked if a team had passed that way,
Without a driver, and astray?
Broke was the deacon's light repose,
Erect upon the bench he rose;
Zeal saw its chance and thus replied,
In phrase not wholly sanctified, —
" Go on still further in your search,
Up to the Universal Church;
You'll find it nowhere else, I swow,
For *everything* ties up there now!"
Some think our race does sinful grow,
That we are frailer than our sires;
But does their view these glimpses show
Of parsons, deacons, and their choirs?

Not wholly wrong the ways of yore,
Nor worthless all the fruit they bore.
When we the old times fairly scan
The types we see of modern man;
His errors dropping one by one,
As fast the circling ages run;
While vices change their shape and hue,
Or old yield places to the new.
Then goodness graced the earth as now;
And meekness with her downcast brow;
Devotion in her closet knelt;
Soft pity human sorrows felt;
While charity found harbor meet,
And gave her benedictions sweet.

Lo! now we see the builders come
To consecrate their Sabbath home;
They fill its spaces with the sound
Of praise spontaneous and profound;
And breathe around its altar fair
Aroma rich of fervent prayer,
Imploring that the Holy One
Will dwell herein their shield and sun.

Have all who shared that season's joy
Passed on where praise has no alloy?
Methinks, if any linger yet,
Waiting for life's pale sun to set,
No brighter mem'ry cheers their way
Than that of this auspicious day.

A pastor now to them is given,
Anointed, blessed, and sent by Heaven;
He comes at manhood's rising morn,
And aims his office to adorn

By word, and deed, from lightness free,
And by thy grace, simplicity.
The sinner's heart he tries to gain,
Not by alarmist's stale refrain;
Nor seeks, through pungent scorn's device,
To break the bigot's shield of ice;
But, seeing in all souls the sign
Of something worthy and divine,
He aims by patient love to win,
And bring his erring brothers in.
Faithful he toils through lengthened years,
With earnest faith, sometimes in tears;
Building on strong foundations laid
By Him who all our ransoms paid.
As in the sacred desk he stands,
His modest mien the heart commands;
And when he spake in truth's defence,
Was heard no stormy eloquence;
In simple phrase his thoughts were dressed,
And gravely, quietly expressed;
Yet reason gave attentive ear,
And guilty conscience could but hear.
His daily walk within his fold,
Of prayer and meditation told;
And touched all hearts to issues higher,
Like David's sweet, immortal lyre.
Beyond his flock the shepherd threw
Influence greater than he knew;
Whose still pulsations over-passed
Sectarian walls so grim and fast,
And prejudice gave way at last.
On gladness' heart he cast no shade,
But sunshine better than it made;
And where pale sorrow wept and moaned,
His voice was heard to comfort toned,

Telling of One now throned on high,
Who tears will wipe from every eye.
To human welfare ever true,
He bridged the gulf 'tween old and new,
By sympathy, with all that's good,
And love baptized in Jesus' blood ;
And thus united youth and age
In life's divinest heritage.
He treads not now our mortal shore ;
But here shall linger evermore,
To keep our hearts from baseness free,
His blest and stainless memory.
Heed well, Mount Auburn, our high trust ;
    In dreamless and untroubled sleep,
Fold to thy breast his precious dust,
    While shade and silence vigil keep !

O ye, ambitious of renown ;
Shouting for men your brows to crown
    With wreaths of fading bay ;
Toiling and struggling here a while,
To gain a monumental pile
    In honor of your clay :

Behold a surer way to fame ;
Behold a fairer, brighter name,
    By gentle goodness won ;
Whose monument in human hearts
Will stand till earth's foundation starts,
    And rayless drops the sun.

O brothers of the sainted dead,
Who bear to men the living bread,
    Pursue your humble way ;

Assured that patient faithfulness
Will win at last divine success,
    Though clouded be your day.

Time glides; now where the good first pastor trod
Another comes to feed the flock of God;
In doctrine sound, — well-furnished in the brain
With all the gifts that logic helps attain;
He proved a foeman valiant in the fight,
With dogmas born of Chaos and old Night.
But brief his stay, — there oped another door,
And through it passed our brother, Asher Moore.

He followed, then, who weaves this shoddy verse;
Let other bards *his* history rehearse, —
Bards who, like Wordsworth, think the *simplest* theme
Will best inspire the high poetic dream.

Who next the burden of the parish took?
One who in air, in attitude, in look
And speech, the consciousness displayed that he
Was called of God a *minister* to be.
He fed the sheep, the tender lambs caressed,
Who rise up now and gladly call him blessed.
For years the West has claimed him as her own,
And proudly bids us mark how he has grown
In mental stature, on her boundless plain,
Where men shoot upward like the corn and grain.
With deep regret we gave him to that sphere;
But Ryder's name is fondly cherished here.

Who now succeeds to field already white?
Behold, he comes in gospel armor bright!
A youth unknown to fame he enters here,
But famous grows as year succeeds to year;

A power the while within this sacred place,
Whose burning words have left a lasting trace;
But, hark! from Brooklyn Heights a "call" is sent,
Which moves — Bartholomew — the eloquent.

He followed last along this honored way,
Whom here you see, the pastor of to-day;
His pleasant brow with vernal hopes aglow,
Though summer's cares their lengthening shadows throw;
Still fresh for toil where tasks are to be done,
As when he first his Master's work begun;
The public's friend — the parish's faithful servant —
By all beloved, — your Patterson the fervent.
God bless him, and the people of his charge,
That Zion's borders here they may enlarge,
While long, in union's strength, they wield their power,
And wide diffuse religion, richest dower.

Fifty years, eventful years, have come and gone,
Since here in faith was laid this corner-stone;
And these fair walls by prayer were set apart
In Christ's dear name, to worship of the heart!
Since then how many feet these aisles have trod,
That walk unsandalled now in courts of God
On high! I see them coming at the call
Of Sabbath bell, that peals alike for all!
The aged come, upon whose locks of gray
The light of suns supernal seems to lay;
And with them walk, erect in manhood's prime,
Their sons, who bear the burdens of the time;
And daughters staid, whose trustful, tender love,
Is purest, ripest for the home above.
The young I see, whose buoyant spirits leap,
Subdued by hours they find it hard to keep;

And in that long procession, here and there,
Move sadly on brows shadowed deep by care ;
And mourners come, in sable weeds of grief,
To here enjoy devotion's sweet relief.

O peaceful aisles ! O walls, and altar dear !
Could you disclose all you have witnessed here,
Since on the air first pealed yon signal bell,
What deep emotions would our bosoms swell !
Here hardened hearts, by grace divine subdued,
Felt the first thrills of love and gratitude ;
And long-lost minds in error's starless night
The fore-gleams caught of truth's redemptive light ;
Here love parental has its offspring brought,
And on its brow God's benediction sought ;
While thanks, by speech unfettered, reached the throne,
For gifts and trusts such love delights to own.
Here hearts have tasted wedlock's earliest joy,
Ere time or change had dashed it with alloy :
Ah, yes ! and hither have been borne the dead,
Around whose forms were burning tear-drops shed,
Even while faith a better world portrayed,
And hope's bright beams lit up the funeral shade !

This olden Fane, within whose hallowed walls
The mem'ries cluster which the hour recalls,
Though voiceless as the spheres we nightly greet,
For many souls has had a language meet,
While here it stood, as years went circling by,
Embodied praise of Love enthroned on high !
More earnest those now battling for the right,
Whose hearts were toned by its inspiring might ;
More ready these, now waiting on the shore,
This world to leave, and cross death's Jordan o'er ;

And rising ranks beyond the darkling wave
Mount higher now for impulse which it gave.
A beacon-light by truth set here of yore,
Its circles bright have widened more and more,
Till far around is seen its pleasant ray,
The pledge and earnest of a coming day,
When hate no more shall curse our struggling world,
And sin and error from their thrones be hurled!

As it *has* stood, for ages may it stand,
Religion's boon to our most favored land, —
Its faithful bell still calling men apart
From things of earth which too much hold the heart;
Its walls inviting weary ones to rest,
Where cares grow lighter on the troubled breast;
Its altar winning souls to pious prayer;
Its organ sounding on the Sabbath air
The strains that teach the worldling's lips to praise,
And in God's house his deep thanksgiving raise:
While points its spire, like faith's own finger bright,
Where move our loved ones in their robes of light;
And where, at last, by Heaven's abounding grace,
We hope to dwell with all our ransomed race.

HYMN.

The Past! Its ways are beaming
   With thy sure mercies, Lord;
Thy truth and grace redeeming,
   Sent o'er the earth abroad,
The hoary shrines of error
   Have cast aside; and free
From darkness, doubt, and terror,
   Its children come to thee.

The Present! Loudly sounding,
   Its cheering tones are heard;
Be our full hearts abounding
   In its strong Hope and Word!
Be strength and wisdom, Father!
   Bestowing what we need,
Truth's harvest-sheaves to gather —
   Christ's kingdom here to speed.

The Future! Indications
   Of mightier works are there, —
Truth's promised revelations;
   Thine arm of power made bare;
From sin's dread reign exemption,
   Man's life in Christ divine;
The erring world's redemption:
   The glory, Father, thine!

PRAYER AND BENEDICTION.

Rev. J. G. BARTHOLOMEW, D. D.

THE CONGREGATION THEN REPAIRED TO THE CHAPEL AND PARTOOK OF A BOUNTIFUL

COLLATION.

THE DIVINE BLESSING WAS INVOKED BY REV. BENTON SMITH, AND AN HOUR WAS PLEASANTLY PASSED IN SOCIAL REUNIONS.

EVENING SERVICES.

ANTHEM.

PRAYER,
By Rev. W. H. Ryder, D. D.

HYMN.

Glorious things of thee are spoken,
    Zion, city of our God !
He whose word cannot be broken
    Formed thee for his own abode.
On the Rock of Ages founded,
    What can shake thy sure repose ?
With salvation's walls surrounded,
    Thou mayst smile at all thy foes.

See ! the streams of living waters,
    Springing from eternal love,
Well supply thy sons and daughters,
    And all fear of want remove.
Who can faint while such a river
    Ever flows their thirst t' assuage ?
Grace, which, like the Lord the giver,
    Never fails from age to age.

Round each habitation hovering,
    See the cloud and fire appear !
For a glory and a covering,
    Showing that the Lord is near.
Fading is the worldling's pleasure,
    All his boasted pomp and show ;
Solid joys and lasting treasure
    None but Zion's children know.

ADDRESS

By Rev. George Putnam, D.D.,

Pastor of the First Parish Church.

My Friends: I feel somewhat embarrassed to say the few words that I have to say. Nevertheless I am too old a soldier to shrink from standing where I am put. I accepted with great pleasure the invitation from your minister to be present here to-night, for, as he has kindly said, I have been here in a neighboring church through almost the entire period of your history, — through more than four-fifths of it certainly. I have known your whole progress; I have been associated more or less, as far as events have allowed, with your ministers.

When I came to the town Dr. Ballou was the minister here. I listened to the beautiful and just tribute to him, in the poem read this afternoon, with pleasure. He welcomed me cordially as a neighbor when I came, and I learned to respect him. I found him then what all know him to have been since. He was a scholar and a Christian, a wise, a prudent, sound, earnest, kindly man, whom I highly esteemed in life, and whose memory I join you in revering.

Of your living ministers, all of whom I have known, and happily known, I may not speak in their presence, except that I must be allowed to say, that amongst the ministers of the many denominations in this town whom I have known, as they have come and gone again, none have stood higher in personal character, and professional fidelity, and devotion to the interests of religion and good morals, — none have stood higher, I say, than your ministers from first to last. And allow me to say of this society, as a near neighbor, — in some sense an outsider, and yet not an outsider altogether and by no means in sympathy, — allow me to say that this parish, as a society, as a body, have held as high a place for the virtues of social life, for order and peaceableness, for honest dealing, for good neighbors, for the domestic virtues, and the virtues of public spirit, for all the virtues that should grace and crown a Christian church, — this parish, I say, has held as high a position as any other in the town. (Applause.) It is not much to say now, you all know it, and the community all know it; but I might remind some of the younger members here, that fifty years ago there was very extensively a doubt through the community whether a Universalist church could maintain all these virtues as high as those churches that retained what used to be called the sanction of morals. It was doubted, when I was a youth, whether good morals and piety would be maintained in a church that rejected the doctrine of everlasting punishment. But those fifty years are gone by, and nobody has any doubts now about it. I say that the Christian morals, rectitude, piety, have had as good a chance of success in a Universalist Society as in any other.

I have witnessed, from a ministry in a near neighborhood, your prosperity with satisfaction and entire sympathy. I have rejoiced in it. I have not been conscious of any antagonism, any rivalry, any separate interest. I consider you on our side; of course I do. (Laughter and applause.) In some sense, and in a larger sense, I say of all the Christian churches, that we are all on one side, on the side of piety and virtue. Yet when we come to a narrower sense, on the side of liberal religion, you and I are one, so far as I see, or understand, or feel. Your denomination and mine, without always knowing it and always feeling it, have always been working towards the same end. Our success is yours, if you did but know it; and yours is ours, and I do know it. (Laughter and applause.) To be sure there is a difference of administration; therefore I am not one to cry aloud for union. It is not necessary for sympathy, for harmony, or for cooperation. You have your history, and you are justly proud of it; you have your methods of organization; you have your associations; you have your calendar, your saint calendar, of great and good men, whose memories you cherish and revere. We have ours. You stick to yours, and we stick to ours; and yet we all mean the same thing, working in different ways.

Let me take the occasion to congratulate you, not only upon your prosperity as an association here, but upon your splendid celebration at Gloucester, the centenary of your denomination. You have a right to be proud of that century of history. You have done a great and good work in the world, as the Methodists have in their century of history; a different one, but equally necessary. You have done a great work in helping to remove from Christian thought and feeling the old dogma that blinded the Christian world for centuries, darkened out the purest and the sweetest light in it, of honest and sincere men, who wanted enlightening. It was a terrible nightmare on the heart and conscience of the world; it made thousands and tens of thousands of noble men and women in the world gloomy, anxious, troubled. I am in doubt whether that doctrine did not produce more misery in the world than it removed or comforted. Your denomination took that doctrine separately; you bore everything against it. That was your work, and a proud work it was. You fought against it till it was everywhere much mitigated, or renounced by great numbers, given up by numbers who retain their good standing in the Orthodox Evangelical denominations, where it is not questioned at all, and where it was held in a mitigated form till it has faded, faded more and more, and is going, going, and at last is gone altogether. (Laughter.) Your denomination have a right to congratulate yourselves on the work done in the century. Let me say for my own denomination, too, that I think we have done just as much. We charged the old system of doctrine right along the whole line; you carried on a more Napoleonic policy, and charged upon a single point. That was for a time, — now large forces are over the field.

We have a different sort of culture, I think. We have done our full share with you, no more, but just as much, in carrying on the work of liberalizing the Christian world and making the gospel glad tidings, and not sad ones. I bid you God-speed just as heartily as I would my own denomination, and I just as much rejoice in your prosperity and success.

I say I have witnessed the administration of all your ministers. Let me say that in your whole fifty years of history you have had as many ministers, less one, as my old church, two hundred and forty years of age, has had from the beginning. Not from any fault of yours or of your ministers, but this is the tendency of the times. I have no criticism to make upon the matter; it is produced by the spirit of the times, and has borne its fruit. As a neighbor and friend I congratulate you. I see you enjoy these proceedings. I see you are happy in reviewing your history. I join with you in perfect sympathy and accord, and God grant you another half century of growth and prosperity till you overrun. Colonize wherever you go; wherever you can, start a new society, and fill it and carry it on, and God go with you and crown all your endeavors. May your next fifty years be as happy and prosperous as your last fifty years have been! (Applause.)

HYMN.

Tune.— Keller's American Hymn.

Children of Light! lift your voices on high!
    Sing ye glad praises to God in this hour;
Voices of mortals to angels reply;
    Sing of his wisdom, and goodness, and power.
Sing of that grace by the Father revealed,
    Grace to no nation or people confined,
Grace in the Son, whom the Father hath sealed,
    Full and complete for the race of mankind!

Praise that through clouds which so heavily hung
    Over the tribes and the nations below,
Shone this glad truth, which the angel-choir sung
    Over still Bethlehem, ages ago :
" Peace on the earth, and good-will to mankind!"
    Truth which all heaven delights to proclaim;
Truth in which mortals exultant shall find
    Highest of glory to God's holy name.

Praise, that this truth through a century gone,
    O'er our broad land hath its radiance shed;
Praise, that its brightness, increasing, shines on,
    Light to the blinded, and life to the dead!
So through all ages its mission shall run,
    Waking glad anthems on earth's farthest shore,
Making the church and humanity one —
    One in Christ Jesus, the Lord evermore!

ADDRESS

Of Rev. Asher Moore,

Pastor from April, 1838, to January, 1839.

My Friends: I have listened with feelings of profound interest to all the exercises of the day. You will suffer me to say that nothing has been more grateful to my feelings than the address you have just listened to from Dr. Putnam. I feel especially the kindly, the neighborly spirit which he has exhibited before you in his very appropriate speech. I learned to respect that man in the early part of my ministry here, and that feeling of respect which I then bore him has been deepened and strengthened at this time.

You will permit me to say that I consider myself very happy that I am permitted to stand once more before you, and to bear a humble part in the services. I cannot but call to my remembrance the time when I first came among you, in fear and in much trembling, a mere stripling of a boy, with his straight, dark hair. And now you see before you a somewhat portly old gentleman with whitened locks, indicating that his career on earth is drawing towards a close. Since I was here among you we have experienced many changes. Some of them have been sad and trying, and if you will allow me to make a little personal reference to myself, I must say that since I was here I have been like one broken upon a wheel, with my bones crushed, and have suffered long and severely. I cannot but call to my remembrance this day a vision which deeply impresses me, and the more so because some of these old and familiar friends, in kindly accosting me, have inquired of me concerning the wife of my youth, not knowing that four years ago this very day her earthly course was closed. And soon after that time I met with a fearful accident, which crippled me for a long time, and from the effects of which I have not yet recovered. During that long season of sorrow, you will not think it strange that I sadly missed the presence of one who was ever ready to minister to my wants, as with the hand of an angel. And I call to remembrance not only that companion of my youthful days, but the fathers and mothers with whom I became acquainted during my short ministry here, thirty years ago. I look through these seats, and miss those faces with which I had become familiar. I think of Stratton, of Burrows, of Bugbee, and many others, and among them, of course, I cannot fail to recall to my mind the saintly, kind-hearted man, Dr. Ballou. Never shall I forget the peculiarly modest gentleness of disposition he exhibited when, on my being invited in my early days to become the pastor of this flock, I deemed it prudent to run over to Medford to consult him on the matter. I questioned him in his study as to the character of the people and the prospects likely to open to the minister who took charge of them. With his peculiar modesty he turned his look upon me and said, "Brother Moore, if there was not vital strength in that society it never could have survived my ministry of seventeen years." I knew how modestly the man spoke, and that very declaration on his part gave to me the assurance that this was the place for me to labor.

I have not forgotten my short pastorate here; I have sometimes regretted that it was not longer continued. But the present pastor of this people in his address stated, properly, that the rigor of the climate was too severe for the young Southern boy, and that there was a feeling of loneliness and homesickness in the wife of his youth, and so, there coming unexpectedly an invitation to settle in Philadelphia, the city of my fathers, where I trace my Quaker parentage, and where I felt I should be at home, the connection between us was severed in a very short time.

Suffer me to refer again to the happy remarks made concerning the feeling which has existed among the several pastors of this church. All are here save one, the greatest of all, the first, who has passed away to his rest. Whilst listening to the address of this afternoon, I could not help wondering,— Is the spirit of that sainted man among us?—and there seemed to pass before my vision a long procession in which he and other good men now gone took part. I was amazed when I heard the declaration that of the original members of this church not one remained. Your fathers, where are they? And the prophets, do they live forever? Who can tell what great changes shall come in the fifty years still before you? But there is one blessed thought coming to us, that the faith you cherish still lives, whilst the fathers and mothers pass away. I think all the venerable fathers in your ministry, every one who labored in the service of the Master when I entered into the vineyard, have passed away. As I looked upon the portrait of one of our departed fathers in a neighboring town, I saw inscribed underneath it, the words, "I have finished my course; I have kept the faith." The words impressed me. This faith lives; it comes to-day with freshness and power to the soul of man. And, my friends, if I were called this night to quit all these earthly scenes, I believe the very last thought that would linger in my mind and would cheer me in my passage through the dark valley of the shadow of death would be " I have kept the faith." I may have been remiss in the performance of duty ; I may have forgotten somewhat my obligations to God and man ; but it is a source of consolation to my mind that no man ever heard me say a word, no man ever knew my pen to write a sentence, in disparagement of the full and perfect claims of the Gospel of the Lord Jesus Christ. We ought to cherish this faith with grateful hearts whilst we live, and bless God for its comforts when death shall come. One of the most pleasing statements I have listened to to-day is that the children have kept the faith of their fathers. I pray God that they may cherish it as the choicest legacy they ever received, and bequeath it unimpaired, undisturbed, as their richest legacy to their children.

But this thought comes into my mind, that others are to succeed me. I am not permitted to speak at any great length, but allow me to express my warm, earnest feeling of rejoicing, that I am permitted to meet you upon this the fiftieth anniversary of the dedication of your church,—a church that presents a youthful and modern appearance compared to the house when I saw it. These changes are indications of the improvement that has taken place among the people. May they all be the means of elevating thought, of rendering devotion more pure and spiritual, and may the God of our fathers meet with the children in this temple of praise, and may His blessing be with you all, henceforth and forevermore. Amen.

ADDRESS

OF REV. W. H. RYDER, D.D.,

Pastor from November, 1849, to January, 1859.

CHRISTIAN FRIENDS: I hold in my hand a printed copy of the sermon preached at the dedication of this house. The sermon was given me, during my residence here, by Mrs. Rumrill. It has upon it the familiar autograph of Dr. Ballou, written by him at my request. "Shall I write Roxbury or Medford?" said he, as he took the pen to write his name. "Roxbury," said I, and so it stands, — "H. Ballou, 2d, Roxbury." How much do you think I would take for this old pamphlet?

1820-1 is a noted year in the history of religious opinions in this town. The First Church, so called, was formed in 1632, some two years after the incorporation of Roxbury. That was the only parish in this neighborhood for nearly one hundred years. Subsequent to this date parishes were formed in what were then remote parts of Roxbury, on the old Dedham road, near the present burial-ground, and one at Jamaica Plain; but these were little more than swarms from the old hive, and were both Congregational in name and sympathy.

Such was the condition of organized religious opinions in this immediate region, until 1820-1, when two parishes were started in Roxbury, both at that time considered heretical, and both largely made up of seceders from the First Church. The Baptist Church was completed a short time before this, and occupied the site of the present First Baptist Church. In a note to the sermon already referred to, there occurs this passage, which is worthy of notice as indicating the generous feeling which actuated the members of the First Parish: "The complacency which the pastors and members of the ancient parishes have exhibited on beholding two new societies springing up at the same time, of a different sect, the first, after a lapse of nearly two centuries, is a proof of the liberality of the age, and demonstrates the excellency of our free institutions."

John Murray moved to Boston Oct. 23, 1793, but he did not preach in Roxbury, so far as I have been able to learn. His meetings in Boston were, however, attended by several persons from this town. In the year 1798, Elhanan Winchester spent a short time in Brookline, with a family named Crehore, — grandparents, I think, of Rev. Joseph Crehore, of our ministry, — and during this visit preached, so far as I know, the first distinctive Universalist sermon ever heard in Roxbury. It was delivered in the First Church, by permission of the pastor. During this visit to Brookline Mr. Winchester also wrote a portion of his reply to "Paine's Age of Reason."

Rev. Hosea Ballou — Father Ballou, as we call him — commenced his ministry in Boston in November, 1817. He was then forty-six years old and a great worker. About a year after his settlement in Boston he began a course of Sabbath evening lectures in Roxbury. His first *sermon* was preached in this city Nov. 29, 1818. After Rev. Paul Dean had succeeded Father Murray in the pastorate of the Hanover Street Church, he assisted Father Ballou in the evening services in Roxbury, preaching ordinarily at alternate meetings. These evening services were continued until the completion of this house; they were held in the Town Hall, where were also held the business meetings of the parish. Mr. Ballou's appointment for Dec. 10, 1820, was filled by a stranger, — a young, awkward, and by no means prepossessing young man, who was understood to be studying with Father Ballou. Good Mother Parker, — now gone to her honored rest, — in speaking to me of that service, said, that " the young man's sermon was about the size of ' Streeter's Hymn Book,' and just about as thick. He blundered badly in his reading," said she, " and we were all glad when he had finished." That young man afterwards became editor and proprietor of the " Trumpet," and, I hardly need add, during the remainder of his life was very influential in the denomination,— Rev. Thomas Whittemore, D. D.

In a little more than six months from the dedication of their house of worship, the members of the parish met to install their first pastor, Rev. Hosea Ballou, 2d. Mr. Ballou was then in his twenty-fifth year. He was called from Stafford, Conn., where he had commenced preaching in his twentieth year. The young pastor began his work at once and in earnest. He had almost everything to do. The affairs of the society not only required his attention, but the unorganized condition of the denomination, and the imperfect state of biblical criticism among his brethren in the ministry elicited his sympathy, and kept him constantly at work. He was a thorough student, both by nature and habit, and soon took the foremost place in the denomination as a clear thinker and trusty scholar.

At the time of Dr. Ballou's settlement here there were

in the United States some fifty preachers of our order. They were for the most part widely separate from each other, connected with small, poor parishes, if settled at all, and everywhere " spoken against." The " General Convention " was then always a memorable occasion. The facilities which now exist for social intercourse were then unknown, so that the preachers seldom met. In the autumn after Mr. Ballou came to Roxbury he attended the Convention, which met that year in Hudson, N. Y. He went in a chaise, accompanied by Father Ballou. They left Roxbury at the close of the morning service on Sunday, and reached Hudson on Tuesday afternoon. The next year Mr. Ballou's name appears among those who attended the convention in Warner, N. H. It was customary, in the early history of this parish, to appropriate thirty dollars, in addition to the regular salary, — the first year, six hundred and fifty dollars and subsequently, for considerable time, seven hundred dollars, — to enable the pastor to represent the parish in the Convention.

In Bro. Patterson's excellent address we were told that the brother who did the glazing for this house is present here to-day. He might also have added that the brother paid for his subscription to the church in work. And there is no doubt that Father Seaver did his work well; but whether he deserves *all* the credit for the durability of the glass is not quite so clear. A part of it, it seems to me, belongs to the boys who have lived hereabouts. I don't think the glass would have stood that long, even if Father Seaver had set them, provided this church had been located in a certain city I know of, a thousand miles away.

The value of an institution to humanity is to be determined both by the quality and extent of the influence which it exerts. The quality of the influence of this parish has been morally healthful from the first. Dr. Ballou differed from some of his brethren as to the prominence which should be given in a religious society to what are called the Christian ordinances. Within five months from his settlement here, he organized a church, thus lifting the important element of religious growth into prominence in the very beginning of the parish. But the doctor did not confine his attention by any means to the ordinances of religion; he was quite as strong in his convictions as to the necessity of correct habits in the community. Intemperance was very prevalent in this section fifty years ago. "Roxbury Neck" was then, and for some time after, a general rendezvous for marketing. A portion of what is called the "Point" was especially riotous and drunken. This, you will all understand, was before the construction of the "Mill Dam," or "Western Avenue." Dr. Ballou found in a layman of the town, Edwin Lemish, a faithful co-worker, and they, for a time, led in the warfare against intemperance and disorder. And so thoroughly did the faithful pastor do his work in this respect, that he impressed his views and feelings upon the entire parish, so that through all its history, the First Universalist Society in Roxbury has been the friend of temperance as well as religion. Indeed, so well did the doctor do his work, so completely did he comprehend what was needful to the upbuilding of a Christian church, that those of us who have succeeded him in the pastorate have had little to do but to follow in his ways of wisdom, and apply the lessons of his example, as advancing years have given opportunity.

An incident occurs to me, which illustrates his insight into character, and his happy use of a fact. In looking over the church records, I observed against the name of one member the word "exsiccated." Surmising what it meant, but not feeling quite certain, I asked Dr. Ballou what a certain member had done, that so hard a word, and one not found in the dictionary, had to be set against his name in the church book. This was the substance of his reply: "That man was converted to Universalism from one of the neighboring churches. He was very zealous; remarkably so. He attended all the meetings, and was very frequently at our house to tea on Sunday night. I soon saw that his zeal was all on the surface, and would soon subside. After a little his attendance at church was less frequent, and finally he disappeared altogether. Exactly what to write on the church book I did not know. He had not withdrawn, nor been dismissed, nor expelled, — his zeal had simply evaporated. So I made up the word, you see." I need only add that exsiccated is from the Latin, exsicco, and signifies to "*dry up*." It seems a pity that so admirable and suitable a word should not come into general use.

Christian Friends: I can say with sincerity that I am grateful that it has been my good fortune to spend ten years of my ministry in this delightful city, as the pastor of this church. I do not regret for a moment that my lot was cast with you for that length of time. In my memory those ten years are luminous with pleasant recollections. I was yet young when I began my ministry here, and quite inexperienced for so responsible a charge. But whether I did as well as I ought, I am confident of having endeavored to do all that I could. My leaving you was a serious experience to me, and tried my sympathies as they had never been tried before. Still, I must with frankness say, that I do not now regret having removed to Chicago. I have had a broad field of labor, and during the eleven years that have intervened since we parted, I have found Chicago a pleasant and happy home. These eleven years have been to me years of hard work, but they have been, nevertheless, years of encouragement, and have brought with them a reasonable amount of personal satisfaction and success.

Since the afternoon service I have been into the house on Vernon street in which I lived so long, and have had the pleasure also of shaking hands with very many of you; and now, as I stand here in this pulpit, and look over this familiar room, and see so many of you still in the very seats you occupied when I used to preach here, it seems almost as if I were back in the old relation, and as if this were really my home. And then, as I consider a moment, and look more carefully over this audience, and remark that those who were children when I left you are now men and women grown, and that many of those who were then elderly are not visibly present here to-day, it is easy to realize that eleven years have passed since I turned my face to the West. Nothing in all the service here to-day has impressed me so much as the cluster of golden Christian fruit gathered in these front pews. Their days well spent — the autumn already come — ripe for heaven! God's blessing upon each one of you, mothers in our Israel! How many times those saintly men, my two good deacons, — Bros. Burrill and Marsh, — have taken the sacred emblem from my hands in front of this altar, and borne them to you and others. Pleasant is the memory of those men as we gather here to-night! Not one of all those named in the Act of Incoporation of this parish, as Bro. Patterson has told you, remains at this present, — death has claimed them all. There were three living eleven years ago, — now the record is closed. Those who have served you as pastors, with the exception of Dr. Ballou (and his widow and two of her daughters we are rejoiced to know are here present), are here to-day, — meeting for the first time and for the *last*, on this common platform.

It gives me pleasure to meet here the honored pastor of the First Church, and to listen to his kind and appropriate address. Aside from all considerations connected with the neighborly kindness which we have respectively received at his hands, as we have come and gone, it is fitting that he, as the successor of Rev. Dr. Porter, should be with us to-day. For when the corner-stone of this edifice was laid, the Rev. Dr. Porter participated in the services, and walked in the procession arm-in-arm with Father Ballou. The interest taken by Dr. Putnam in these celebration services completes the fifty years of neighborly sympathy and Christian intercourse.

There are many topics on which I would be glad to say a word, but I am admonished that the time is short, and that there is much yet to be said by others. I call to mind, as active in my day here, the honored " Samaritan Society," the " Literary Union," the " Mechanics' Association," which, as an outside organization, was the source of great good in the place. I think of the generous aid given me by many young men, now in the strength of their years, and of many noble helpers whose names I will not mention, but whose images are in my mind. And, as I conclude this address, allow me to suggest that the occasion, however interesting in itself, cannot be in the highest sense a success, if it make no healthful impression upon our minds and hearts. Shall all these memories awakened to-day pass from us as a pleasant dream, or will we use them as aids in quickening and ennobling our lives? I have endeavored, in what I have said, to show you wherein Dr. Ballou's ministry was so fruitful in good. He *began* right; he laid a solid and sure foundation; he turned the hearts of the people, in the very beginning of their parish work, to the necessity of personal religion Are there not some here now who need to hear this lesson?

Are there not some here, — some who are still young, — whose hearts are not yet fixed in truth and duty, who will apply this noble example to themselves? We look back now to the day of dedication. Some who are here remember the impression made upon their lives by the services of that time. Fifty years hence some of you will look back upon this semi-centennial celebration; and may God grant, that to all of you who may then be alive, the retrospect may be one of satisfaction and good cheer.

ADDRESS

Of Rev. J. G. Bartholomew, D. D.,

Pastor from July, 1860, to January, 1866.

Friends: I need not tell you that I am glad to be here on this occasion ; you all know that. My heart rejoices as I stand once more in this familiar place, and see before me the faces that have greeted me here so often in those happy days gone by. I feel as one that has been long absent, returned again to the old home.

I have listened with a great deal of satisfaction to what has been said this afternoon of the early history of this parish, and I have learned many things that I did not know before. But nothing that I have heard has made me feel a deeper affection for you than that which I shall always carry in my heart. Brother Patterson has told us something of the spirit of the fathers who laid the foundations of this church half a century ago ; who gave so liberally of their time, their money, and their thought, for the upbuilding of our cause in those times, when it cost more to be a Universalist than it does to day. I was deeply touched by the story of their heroic struggle, and I bear witness to the

truth of his statement, that the same spirit that animated the hearts of the fathers is in the children also.

My knowledge of this society and its affairs dates back to the time immediately following the resignation of Brother Ryder as its pastor. I was then living in a western city, and when the parish began to look about for another minister, to my great astonishment, they came to the very city where I lived. They asked a young man, preaching there, to come down and supply their pulpit for a Sunday or two. I came with that young minister on his first visit to Roxbury. I heard his first sermon in this pulpit; I was with him when he received the unanimous invitation to assume the pastorate here. I shall never forget his reply when the committee pressed him to accept their invitation. "I dare not answer you now," he said; "I must go home and consult my people first." To all their arguments this was his reply. At last they gave him ten days in which to make up his mind. I returned with him to his western home, and I know the struggle that took place in those ten days. His parish gathered around him, insisting upon his giving up all thought of leaving them. They held out many inducements for him to remain, and finally they prevailed. It was no ordinary struggle through which that young man passed. His love for his people wrestled with the great temptation to come to you, with this grand old church and your great warm hearts. I remember how his hand trembled when he wrote to thank you for your confidence and kindness, and tell you that he felt compelled to decline your very flattering invitation. It was a load off his heart when that letter was mailed, for then he supposed the matter was at an end. But he did not know you. The spirit of the fathers was in the children, and no such trifle would be allowed to block their way. Early one morning, as we looked out the window, we saw two of the Standing Committee from Roxbury coming up the street. The young man trembled, for he feared that he was going to be taken by storm. What could he say to them but what he did say, — "Get the consent of my parish, and I will accept your call to Roxbury." It was a bold thing to do, but it shows the earnest spirit of this people, of which no better representatives could be selected than those two men.* They met the trustees of that western church ; they labored long and faithfully ; they gained their point, and telegraphed home the brief but comprehensive message, "All right." Now I am not saying that the fish when caught was worth all this bait ; I am only speaking of the fact to illustrate that spirit of earnestness and persistence that knows no defeat in a good cause, underlying this whole parish.

There is a kind of heroism in that manner of doing things that is admirable. It reminds me of an instance during the Rebellion. While the battle of Shiloh was raging, a Dutch officer rode furiously up to Gen. Grant, and touching his cap, said, " Sheneral, I vants to make von report : Schwartz's Battery is took."—"Ah!" says Grant; "how was that?"— " Vell, you see, Sheneral, de sheshenists come up in front of us, and de sheshenists flanked us, and de sheshenists come in de rear of us, and Schwartz's Battery was took."—" Well, sir," said the General, "you of course spiked the guns?"— " Vat!" exclaimed the Dutchman, in astonishment, "schpike dem guns ? schpike dem new guns ? No ! it would schpoil dem !"—" Well," said the General, sharply, "what did you do?"—" Do? vat did we do ? vy, we took dem back again !" And so it proved. Surrounded by the enemy, they had been compelled to yield up their guns, and then, like heroes,

---

* Hon. GEORGE FROST and ANDREW W. NEWMAN.

as they were, had dashed into the very face of death, and, at the price of many precious lives, brought their battery back. It is that spirit, friends, that makes any cause successful. Wherever a company of men are really in earnest about a matter they will achieve victory somehow. And that has been, in a large measure, the secret of this society's success.

But it has not been *earnestness*, alone, that has built up this large and flourishing parish. The men and women who have wrought here have always taken broad and generous views of things. This church building is a witness to that fact. It has always been a matter of wonder to me that the fathers should build such an edifice as this, — so ample in its proportions, and on such a delightful spot. Why, those were the days of small things! Universalism was then struggling to get a foothold, and it had to contest every step of its advance. Did the fathers look with prophetic vision through these fifty years of achievement, and build for our day instead of theirs? It would seem so. At any rate, there was nothing narrow in their thought. And since their day the same spirit has prevailed. This grand faith of ours has found men and women here who could appreciate its broad and generous and humane suggestions, and from first to last they have labored to carry them out. Whatever measures would promote the interests of our cause, as the history to which we have just listened shows, it has always been the aim of this society to adopt.

And then there is another fact that we are to remember. As Brother Ryder has said, this parish was started right to begin with. Dr. Ballou was a peculiar man in this, that while he was one of our profoundest thinkers, and one of our most finished writers, he was always simple as a child. I have heard him speak on various occasions, and I have read his writings with a great deal of care; but I never heard a sentence from his lips, I never read a sentence from his pen, that was spoken or written for buncombe. He never rode a "hobby." And these two facts are of more importance than we are apt to think. In building up a church there is nothing like plain and simple statements of God's truth. The soul grows by what it feeds upon, and it needs a change of diet as much as the body does. How many churches we have all known, that have died of *spiritual scurvy*, as the result of too frequent swallowing of the same idea! If we are to have a liturgy, let us put in this petition in good plain type: "From all ministers with hobbies, good Lord, deliver us." For the first seventeen years of its existence this church enjoyed the ministry of one of the purest, truest men, that ever stood in a pulpit to break to the people "the bread of life." The stamp of that good man's life and ministry is on the parish yet; and every man who has succeeded him here has felt the influence of it. The memory of him is like a continual benediction. Now a church with such a beginning, unless the children prove utterly recreant and forgetful, cannot but thrive and prosper.

But there is one other element in this society that has done very much towards its healthy growth, and that is its missionary spirit. It is an ordinance of God, that prosperity shall come in at the door when we carry blessings out to others. No man, no community, no church, can hope for any large success, that lives for self alone. "It is more blessed to give than to receive," is illustrated by everything around us. The root labors for the stem, and the stem for the leaf, and the leaf for the flower and fruit. And when the leaf has completed its work it falls to the ground, to cover the root from the winter's frost, and gives back of its substance, through decay, that which it received. The mountain spring makes contribution to the sea, and the sea sends back its messengers of cloud to fill the cup again, and on their way they scatter blessings on the grass and corn, and give refreshment to the wayside flower. And it is just as true in the moral world as it is in the material, that blessings come of blessings. The law of God is, that a church that gives freely of its substance, to help other churches, to build up worthy institutions, to carry out reforms, to feed the hungry, and clothe the naked, shall gain strength thereby for its own home work. The Methodist denomination furnishes a striking illustration of this fact. That sect is a perfect marvel of success. Wherever you look you will see a Methodist church or chapel, and whenever you listen you will hear their grand old hymns. Now this astonishing growth is not because of its theology, by any manner of means; it is not because of its peculiar organization, or its enthusiasm and zeal, although these have been great helps; but because that sect has been pushing out its boundary lines continually. It has been willing to go down and labor for the poor and the neglected. They have done the work that others have so largely overlooked, and consequently they have triumphed gloriously, while those sects that have devoted their energies chiefly to looking after the upper classes, and building up an aristocracy of religion, have hardly held their own. It seems strange that this secret of power and of success is not more generally recognized by Christian societies; that our denomination, especially, has so long stood idle in the market-place when God has been saying to us, "Go into the vineyard." This parish has been greatly blessed, and largely, I believe, because it has always been willing to "lend a hand" in every good work. My ministry among you was at a time that gave me an opportunity to see this spirit tested. I came to you just at the time when threats of secession filled the air. I was with you when the storm of rebellion burst upon the land with all its fury. I stood here to counsel you through all those terrible years of sacrifice and sorrow. I saw your husbands, your sons, and your brothers go forth with your blessing to meet the dangers of the battle-field, and give their lives, if need be, to maintain the nation's honor. I see here to-night young men whose hearts were fired with patriotic zeal in those dark days, and whose willing sacrifices I shall never forget. I stood with you by those open graves, when your eyes were brimming with tears, and your hearts were almost broken with grief, to tell you of God's truth and love, and bid you put your trust in Him. I know how deeply you were tried and with what heroic spirit you bore it. I shall never forget the generosity with which you gave of your means whenever the country could be helped thereby. I never appealed to you in the name of justice and humanity in vain. I never asked you to aid in any denominational work that you did not readily and gladly respond. And to this spirit I attribute very much of your success.

But I am claiming your attention too long. I only wanted to join with my brethren here in telling you how much I rejoice in your prosperity, and how precious to me are the memories of those years in which we labored together. Brethren, the history of fifty years of labor and achievement is before us. You know what the fathers did, you know what you have accomplished, and you know what still remains to be done. If there is any obstacle in your way, this is the time to remove it. If there are any figures on the blackboard that you would be glad so see erased, now is the time to take the sponge and wipe them out. If there is any burden of debt, cast it off to-night that you may enter upon this new half century unincumbered and free.* This church has a great mission to accomplish yet, and it cannot afford to carry any useless weight. The influence of our blessed faith is spreading wider and wider every year. The world is coming more and more to appreciate our work; old prejudices are giving way before the advancing light; bigotry is giving place to Christian fellowship, and men of every sect and creed are beginning to say, though as yet in a whisper, —

> "I think Heaven will not shut forevermore,
> Without a knocker left upon the door,
> Lest some belated wanderer should come,
> Heart-broken, asking just to die at home,
> So that the Father will at last forgive,
> And looking on his face that soul shall live.
>
> "I think there will be watchmen through the night,
> Lest any, far off, turn them to the light;
> That he who loved us into life must be
> A Father infinitely fatherly,
> And groping for him, these shall find their way,
> From outer dark, through twilight, unto day."

* At the close of Mr. Bartholomew's address, the pastor said that at the last Annual Meeting the Treasurer's report showed that the parish was in debt $15,000. Since that time this sum had been reduced to $6,000. It was not intended when the $9,000 was subscribed to attempt more at present. But he could not believe the parish was willing to enter upon the work of the *next half century* with any such incubus upon it. A collection was at once taken, which, together with a contribution on a subsequent Sunday morning, amounted to $7,500, and the debt was more than provided for.

HYMN.

Marching on, marching on, in the years that are gone,
    The glad train of pilgrims by faith we behold,
And the sheen of their robes is the jubilee-dawn
    That bursts through the gates of the city of gold.
Marching on, marching on,
Shout the triumph-cry, shout the triumph-cry,
Marching on, marching on,
Shout the victory! the victory! the victory!!
Marching on, etc.

Pressing on, praying on, in the vesture of clay,
    With sandals and staff and the voice of a psalm,
We follow that train to the portals of day,
    The kingdom and glory of God and the Lamb.
Marching on, etc.

Pressing on toward the mark by a hallowing faith,
    Communion we hold with the pilgrims of yore,
For the paths that lead down to the shadow of death
    Lead upward and onward to life evermore.
Marching on, etc.

ADDRESS

By Rev. Benton Smith,

Formerly a member of the Parish.

Christian Friends: The striking of that clock sounds much as it did in years long gone by, and the late hour warns me to be very brief. I have nothing but a child's story to tell you. It is full forty-five years since my childish feet first trod the floor of this church,—about five years after its dedication. Although some of these former pastors, who seem to be elderly men, have spoken to you of being here thirty years ago, I feel quite old to-night when I remember that I was here fifteen years before them. I remember this church as it was, with its uncarpeted floor, its high pulpit, its stove-pipes carried through the windows upon either side, because the house was built without chimneys. I can remember carrying the foot-stove into our pew for mother and sisters. How well I recall the familiar scene of the loved pastor of those days coming up the centre aisle, introducing his family to their pew, and then disappearing through that mysterious door which led to the large and wonderful pulpit!

Since the zeal and energy with which the society always

conducted its affairs have been alluded to here to-day, I may mention, as instances of it, the grand vocal and instrumental music which was always provided for the public worship, and the elaborate and beautiful manner in which, for many years, the church was adorned at Christmas time.

Had I time I could continue telling you of the events of those years. But you will ask me what influence this church and its services exerted upon me. I remember very distinctly some of the sermons preached by Dr. Ballou. It seems to me that my eyes could not have been removed from him, as on one Sunday he preached from the words, "We love Him, because He first loved us;" for his words touched my heart, and their sound seems to linger here, although it must be more than forty years since they were spoken. Allusion has been made to the fact, that Dr. Ballou organized a church soon after he assumed the pastoral charge here. Upon the first Sunday of each month we saw the table spread here for the Lord's supper, and the sight of it blessed us. On one of those Sundays five of us children wended our way of two miles towards home, along what you call Shawmut Avenue, but what we called the Turnpike then, and talked together of the communion table, the emblems upon it, the purpose of the sacrament, and of how happy we should be could we participate in the communion. I may ascribe much of what I am to-day to the Christian teachings and example of Dr. Ballou which blessed my early years. I have treasure here to-night which has not faded away. I have treasure here to-night which has increased as the years have rolled on. None can steal it. Moth and rust cannot corrupt it. And, in conclusion, I will say to fathers and mothers, come here and gather treasures which you may impart to your children. I would urge the young men and young women to be constant attendants upon the services here; I would urge the children to come upon every returning Sabbath, and in after years they will possess treasure that nothing earthly can give. And now, as, after so many years of absence, I have come back to dwell close to the old church again, and to have the church of my boyhood the Sunday home of my family, I cannot tell you how glad and thankful I am that this church was a familiar place to me in childhood and youth, and that the memory of those far-off years comes to me beautiful in Christian light.

ADDRESS

By Rev. Henry Blanchard,

Formerly a member of the Parish and Sunday School.

Good Friends: I always liked Brother Smith, and now I know something of the reason. It is, in part, because we were boys together in this old church and Sunday school. I did not know the fact till the other night, when Brother Patterson asked me to attend this pleasant half-century meeting. When he was speaking, I could see the old seat up there in the gallery where I used to sit when I was a boy, and the pew down there, which once was Brother Fay's, where, with my grandmother, I also had a seat very often. I can remember to-night one of Brother Fay's sermons which I heard in those days long since passed away. It was about the roses that fade. Especially do I remember one Sunday afternoon, when the good pastor came into our school, put his hand kindly upon my head, and said some gentle words. I have often felt that touch, in imagination, since then, and sometimes, when the thought has come to me in my own ministry, "What good does it do to speak to the little ones?" the knowledge of the impression made upon a "little one" by the pastor's voice and hand, has made me feel that a great deal of good is accomplished in this way.

It is interesting to me to remember to-night that the first time I ever "spoke in public" was in this town of Roxbury. I went to the old school-house on this street (pointing to the left), and one day the master called for volunteers to speak. The boys sitting in my row all said they would be ready, and so, unwilling to be different, but fearful of the task, I, too, volunteered. Henry Williams came for me on the eventful night, and before the few companions, I " spoke my piece."

When Brother Ryder was speaking, he thrilled me through and through. Let me ask your attention, therefore, to some thoughts which are responsive to his own. Speaking only as a young man, as one who has seen some little of life even though he is yet young, as one who is proud to think that he was once the pupil of good Dr. Ballou, let me say to the young men who are before me that there are three things concerning which I beseech them to think with the most earnest thinking. The first is, that without God, our Father, we are nothing in this world. I have crossed the sea and stood in France; I have seen the stars shining over the waters for fifty nights of the passage from Havre to New Orleans; I have seen the great West, travelling many a mile over its broad surface; I have felt the peril of position, afloat on the ocean, or shut up in railway car. The thought which has come to me, with power to comfort, is, that God my Father rules over all, and I can put my trust in Him;" and the blessed words have rung and rung in my mind, "When my father and my mother forsake me, then the Lord will take me up." O young men, young men who are in this church to-night, believe me, it is the crowning glory of your manhood to believe in God, to put your trust in Him, to feel His presence everywhere, and to know that you can be strong and manly only as you love and serve Him with all your souls!

My second thought is that we are to rejoice in the leadership of Jesus of Nazareth. The older I grow, young friends, the more does this teacher appear to me worthy of our love and homage. Striving to know something of philosophy, studying history with earnestness, I believe that this man had the spirit of God as none other ever did. There are those who demand precise definition of the phrase "leadership of Jesus,"—who are very suspicious of certain declarations, fearing that they indicate a lack of homage for Jesus. Let me ask you to be free from others' interpretations,—to study the world's need of a great example,—to consider that only the divine passion of love of God and man is a power mighty enough to bring the world to a higher level. As you study history, I think you will be very likely to believe that God has inspired many teachers; that in no country and no age has he been without his prophets. I believe just as strongly, that, comparing this prophet, this Son of God, with others, you will see that his teachings are completer, grander, than those of any other single leader, and that his spirit is indeed of God. I entreat you to love him, to honor him, to study his words, to imitate the spirit of his life.

My last thought is, that young men should belong to the church. For myself, I see but one. It is composed of all those who, loving God and man, take Jesus as the great helper to this divine life. I see therefore no Universalist church, nor Episcopalian church, but the one society of Jesus, "which is the church of Christ." I believe mightily in this, as the divinest instrument to redeem the world. Learning, with all its colleges, cannot do it. Neither Literature, nor Art, can accomplish it. Only as men are born into the kingdom of love, and so see the greatness of Jesus, is it possible for this world to be lifted from its low level to the height which God means it to reach. We read that the Venetian merchants put the head of Christ upon their coins; so, to-day, I would have young men stamp the image of Jesus upon all they do and give, — on their deeds and on their money. It is very pleasant to me to see young men joining this great Christian society. I rejoice in the old companionship with young men in this city who give their time, money, abilities, to the church. I rejoice in my dear friend Henry Metcalf, — in Henry Williams, — in John Joy, and others. I would that hundreds would do as these are doing. If you have talents, young men, if you have learning, if you have wealth, give these, give these to this society of Jesus, and on this grand occasion — the fiftieth anniversary of this church, — consecrate yourselves anew to the service of God and man.

HYMN.

Hail, sweetest, dearest tie that binds
    Our glowing hearts in one ;
Hail, sacred hope, that tunes our minds
    To sing what God hath done.
It is the hope, the blissful hope,
    Which gospel grace hath given :
The hope, when days and years are past,
    We all shall meet in heaven.

From eastern shores, from northern lands,
    From western hill and plain,
From southern climes, the brother-bands
    May hope to meet again ;
It is the hope, the blissful hope,
    Which love divine hath given :
The hope, when life and time are o'er,
    We all shall meet in heaven.

No hope deferred, no parting sigh,
    That blessed meeting knows ;
There friendship beams from every eye,
    And hope immortal grows.
It is the hope, the precious hope,
    Which boundless grace hath given :
The hope, when time shall be no more,
    We all shall meet in heaven.

PRAYER AND BENEDICTION,

By the Pastor.

APPENDICES.

APPENDIX A.

DECLARATION OF FAITH.

UNITING COMPACT AND GOVERNMENT OF THE CHURCH.

DECLARATION OF FAITH.

We, the subscribers, believing in Jesus of Nazareth as the all-sufficient Saviour, and being fully persuaded that his gospel is the word of God, and the perfect rule of faith and practice, do feel it our duty to make a public declaration of our faith, and to unite ourselves as a Church of Christ, or Company of Believers in the Gospel, that we may the better enjoy, practise, defend and support the Christian Religion.

Therefore, after serious consideration, we adopt the following Declaration of Faith, as expressive of the fundamental articles of our religious belief, and as containing truths, the knowledge of which is essential to the Christian character.

We believe that there is One God; and that in the Scriptures of the Old and New Testaments he has given a revelation of his character, of the mission of his Son Jesus Christ, and of the duty and final destination of mankind. And we believe that the happiness of all rational creatures depends immediately on their obedience or holiness.

UNITING COMPACT.

Acknowledging Jesus Christ to be the Head of the Church, and submitting ourselves unto him as such, we do hereby, as before him, agree to meet together, on the first day of the week, for the public worship of God, the breaking of bread, the reading of the Scriptures, and the Preaching of the Gospel; that we may render becoming homage to our Creator, enliven our faith, improve ourselves in holiness, and strengthen our fellowship with each other; and that we may assist in bringing up the youth in the nurture and admonition of the Lord, in making them acquainted with the Scriptures, and in inspiring them with the love of virtue.

We will endeavor to abstain from every vice, and faithfully to practise all the virtues of the Christian Religion. As far as in us lieth, we will live peaceably with all men.

And now, commending ourselves and all mankind unto God, to whom we are responsible, and on whom we are entirely dependent for all that light, wisdom and direction which we need, we pray that he would be pleased to make additions to the Church, of such as shall be saved from the evil that is in the world, by believing and obeying the truth as it is in Jesus; and that, by his grace, he would enable us, in all things, to conduct according to our Christian profession.

PLATFORM.

Organization of the Church.

ART. I. OFFICERS.

The standing officers of this Church shall be a Moderator, two or more Deacons, a Treasurer, and a Clerk; all of whom, except the Moderator, shall be elected by ballot. The Deacons, when chosen, shall be entitled to their office during good behavior; the Treasurer and Clerk during one year, reckoned from the time of their election.

ART. II. MODERATOR.

The minister settled over this Church and the Society with which it is connected shall be, *ex officio*, Moderator; but in his absence, the Clerk may call the Church to order for the choice of a Moderator for the time; and also in the absence of the Clerk, another shall be chosen to fill his office *pro tem*.

ART. III. DEACONS, ETC.

The duties of the Deacons shall be such as usually devolve on their office; the duty of the Treasurer shall be to receive and keep all moneys committed to his care by the Church, or for the use of the Church, to pay them out at its direction, and to keep a faithful account of the receipts and payments of the Treasury; the duty of the Clerk shall be to keep a true record of the transactions and votes of the Church.

Art. IV. Pastoral Committees.

The Church shall be divided into the following Pastoral Committees, which shall be appointed by the Pastor and Deacons, at the annual meeting of the Church; viz.: Committee on the Sick; Committee on Benevolence; Committee on Hospitality; Committee of Visitation; Committee on Sunday Schools and Missions.

Art. V. Duties of Pastoral Committees.

Section 1. The Committee on the Sick shall visit the sick in their respective districts, provide watchers when needed, do all in their power to make the sick comfortable, and report the cases to the Pastor.

Sect. 2. The Committee on Benevolence shall devise, and put in operation, such means as they may deem suitable to reach and help the needy, especially of the household of faith. They shall also endeavor to provide employment for those who are seeking it.

Sect. 3. The Committee on Hospitality shall seek out the strangers in the parish, call upon them, introduce them to the Pastor and members of the congregation, and endeavor to make them feel that they are among friends.

Sect. 4. The Committee of Visitation shall endeavor to make the acquaintance of all the members of the congregation who reside in their respective districts, call upon every person, and exert themselves to unite the parish as one great family.

Sect. 5. The Committee on Sunday Schools and Missions shall be charged with the superintendence of these great departments of Christian work in the parish. They shall visit the Sunday School as often as once a quarter, and report on its condition at the quarterly meetings of the Church. They shall also interest themselves in the establishment of Mission Sunday Schools, distribution of tracts and books, and in all other work which relates to the spread of the Gospel and the good of souls.

Sect. 6. The Pastoral Committees shall be ready to report at any regular meeting of the Church, at the request of the presiding officer.

Art. VI. Admission of Candidates.

Sect. 1. No candidate shall be admitted as a member of this Church, but by a majority of votes in a regular Church meeting.

Sect. 2. Any person designing to become a member of this Church shall make application to the Pastor, or one of the Deacons; and after the application has been before the Church at least three weeks, the candidate may be received into fellowship on receiving the votes of two-thirds of the members present at any regular meeting. And when the person so elected, shall have signed the Declaration of Faith and Uniting Compact, he or she shall be entitled to a certificate of membership, signed by the Pastor and Clerk. But in case of sickness or unexpected removal from the place, any person may become a member of the Church without presenting the name as above specified, provided the officers are agreed as to the propriety of receiving such person into membership.

Sect. 3. When a candidate shall produce a recommendation from a regular Church, and request an immediate admission, the Church may act on the request in the first regular meeting in which it is brought forward.

Sect. 4. Any member who wishes to withdraw from the Church, by making his or her request known in writing to the Pastor or either of the Deacons, shall have the privilege of so doing ; and on thus withdrawing, shall be entitled to a CERTIFICATE OF CHURCH STANDING from the Clerk, or to a Letter of Recommendation to any other Christian Church, provided he or she has uniformly sustained a good moral character.

Sect. 5. Every candidate, on admission, shall sign the Declaration of Faith.

ART. VII. THE ORDER FOR RECEIVING MEMBERS.

[*When the Church is assembled for communion, all who are to be received shall present themselves before the altar, when the Pastor shall address them as follows ; or he may use such formula as his judgment and taste approve, provided they are not in conflict with the spirit of this formula :* —]

Dearly beloved, on profession of your faith in the Lord Jesus Christ, your desire to learn of him, and to co-operate with us in the study and practice of religion, we gladly receive you into our number. We welcome you to this communion of Christian souls. We earnestly desire to sympathize with you, and will endeavor to watch over and support you in the trials of life, and the work of duty. And may God our Father grant that this union formed on earth may continue in heaven, and fit us for the fellowship of the saints in light.

[*Then all of them in order, kneeling before the minister, he shall baptize those who have not been baptized, saying,*]

N. I baptize thee in the Name of the Father, and of the Son, and of the Holy Spirit. Amen.

[*After that, he shall lay his hands on the head of every one severally, saying,*]

Defend, O Lord, this thy child (or, this thy servant) with thy heavenly grace; that *he* may continue thine forever, and daily increase in thy Holy Spirit, more and more, until *he* come into thy everlasting kingdom. Amen.

[*Then the minister may say,*]

The Lord be with you.

Answer. And with thy spirit.

APPENDICES.

Minister. Our help is in the Name of the Lord;
Answer. Who hath made heaven and earth.
Minister. Blessed be the Name of the Lord;
Answer. Henceforth, world without end.
Minister. Lord, hear our prayers;
Answer. And let our cry come unto thee.

[*Then the Lord's Prayer shall be said, minister and people repeating it together, all reverently bowing the head, or kneeling.*
Then the minister may offer Prayer in his own words.
Then shall follow the Benediction :]

The grace of our Lord Jesus Christ, and the love of God, and the fellowship of the Holy Spirit be with us all evermore. Amen.

[*The above order may be preceded by singing, by the Church, two verses of the hymn, beginning,*

"Come in, thou blessed of the Lord."

and, at the close of the ceremony, the closing verse of the same hymn may be sung.]

ART. VIII. GOVERNMENT OF THE CHURCH.

Sect. 1. Each member shall be entitled to one vote in all the votes taken in the Church.

Sect. 2. The Church may, in any regular meeting, with the consent of two-thirds of the members present, make such by-laws for its government as it shall judge expedient; provided such by-laws be not inconsistent with the principles of this platform.

Sect. 3. There shall be an Annual Meeting of the Church on the evening of Monday following the first Sabbath in December, for the examination of the accounts and records of the Treasurer and Clerk, for the election of Officers, and for the transacting of any other necessary business.

Sect. 4. The regular meetings of the Church shall be appointed, for the succeeding year, at each Annual Meeting.

Sect. 5. The ordinance of the Lord's Supper shall be administered to the Church as often as a majority of its officers may deem proper.

Sect. 6. Any member who habitually absents himself or herself from the stated observance of the Lord's Supper, for the term of one year, except on account of sickness, old age, absence from town, or some such sufficient reason, shall be considered as withdrawing his or her connection from the Church.

ART. IX. DISCIPLINE OF THE CHURCH.

Sect. 1. This Church disclaims all authority to pass any further judgment against an offender than the mere withdrawing of fellowship.

Sect. 2. The Church shall not withdraw its fellowship from any member without previously giving notice, if possible, to him or her, of the intention.

Sect. 3. If a member shall be guilty of conduct which is inconsistent with the Christian religion, the Church may undertake such labors as it shall judge conducive to reformation; and if those labors prove ineffectual, it shall withdraw its fellowship from the disorderly member.

Sect. 4. When cases of personal difficulty between the members shall arise, the direction given by Christ in the 15th, 16th, and 17th verses of the 18th chapter of Matthew, shall be the rule of procedure.

Art. X. Special Rules.

At the Regular Meetings of the Church, the following order shall be observed:—

1. Singing, reading of the Scriptures, and prayer.
2. Reading the records of the previous meeting.
3. Names of candidates for membership, given by the pastor.
4. Reports of Committees, which shall be introduced successively, in the following order:—

The Pastor, or the Deacon who occupies the chair, shall say:—

Does any one present know of any Member of the Church or Parish who is sick, or in trouble?

This question will call for the Report of the Committee on the Sick, or a response from some member who may know of a case of sickness.

Does any one present know of any Member of this Church or Parish who is in need?

This question will call for a Report from the Committee on Benevolence, mentioning the fact simply that there are cases of poverty, and reporting more fully in private to the Pastor, and to such Members of the Church as may be necessary.

Does any one present know of any stranger who desires to attend our Church, or of any one who has recently come amongst us?

This question will call for the Report from the Committee on Hospitality, or some response from members of the Church.

Does any one present know of any one now connected with this Church or Parish, who ought to be brought into more intimate relations with us as a Christian people?

This question will call for a Report from the Committee of Visitation, or a response from some Member.

APPENDICES. 99

Has any one present anything to say for the good of the young of our Parish, for the good of the Sunday school, or in behalf of Missions?

This question will call for a Report from the Committee on Sunday schools and Missions.

5. Remarks from the Pastor, or from any member present, concerning the general good of the Church, and the comfort and edification of souls.

6. Hymn, Prayer, Benediction.

ART. XI. ALTERATIONS.

This Platform may be altered in any regular meeting of the Church, by a vote of two-thirds of the members present, after notice of the proposed alterations shall have been given in the preceding regular meeting.

NOTE.—The above Declaration of Faith, Uniting Compact, and Platform, stand substantially as when adopted January 4, 1822. What relates to Pastoral Committees, also the order for receiving members, and the Special Rules, were added in 1867.

NAMES OF THE ORIGINAL MEMBERS OF THE CHURCH.

Hosea Ballou, 2d, Pastor.
Elisha Wheeler.
Mark P. Sweat.
Isaac W. Field.
Joanna Field.
Warren Marsh.
Hannah Marsh.
Samuel S. Williams.
Joseph James.
Mary James.
Sally Stratton.
Joseph Stratton.
Wm. J. Newman.
Sarah Newman.
Eliphalet Everett.
Eliza Everett.
Martha Richardson.
Betsey Blackman.
James Blackman.
Josiah Seavernse.
Lewis Morse.
Susan Morse.
Joshua Sampson.
Polly Williams.
Timothy Gay.
Susanna Gay.
Jonathan Williams.
Mary Cook.

APPENDIX B.

SIGNERS OF THE ACT OF INCORPORATION.

William Hannaford.
Elisha Wheeler.
Samuel S. Williams.
Haman Brown.
Charles Joy.
Samuel Parker.
Harford Morse.
Luther Morse.
Lewis Morse.
Joseph Stratton.
Joshua Sampson.
Robert Edwards.
W. J. Newman.
Joseph James.
Mark P. Swett.
Ebenezer Brewer.
Jesse Jordan.
Frederick Chandler.
Opher Haynes.
Isaac Gale.
Warren Marsh.
Joel W. Gay.

Jesse Brown.
Jane Cheney.
Jonathan Williams.
Joseph May.
Aaron White Bugbee.
Lott Young.
Ebenezer Goddard, Jr.
James Riley.
William Cobb.
Eleb Faxon.
Thomas Mayo.
William Dove.
Aaron Bartlett.
Samuel Langley.
William Lingham.
Benjamin Myrick.
John Bodge.
Josiah Richardson.
Luther Newell.
Elisha Whitney.
Enoch Davenport.

APPENDICES. 101

APPENDIX C.

CLERKS OF THE PARISH.

Luther Newell, 1821 to 1822.
Eben. Brewer, 1822 to 1826.
Josiah Bugbee, 1826 to 1838.
Geo. B. Davis, 1838 to 1840.
Calvin Brown, March to Oct. 1840.
Charles Marsh, 1840 to 1850.
Joseph H. Streeter, 1850.

CLERKS OF THE CHURCH.

Joseph James, 1822 to 1837.
E. G. Scott, 1837 to 1840.
Dudley Williams, 1840 to 1841.
A. W. Newman, 1841 to 1851.
Thad's C. Craft, 1851 to 1861.
E. T. Danforth, 1861 to 1863.
A. C. Anderson, 1863.

DEACONS OF THE CHURCH.

Elisha Wheeler, 1821 to 1838.
Mark P. Sweat, 1821 to 1838.
Joseph Stratton, 1838 to 1846.
Benjamin Burrill, 1838 to 1865.
Nathan Watson, 1846 to 1855.
Warren Marsh, 1855 to 1863.
Hosea B. Stiles, 1860.
A. C. Anderson, 1860.
E. T. Danforth, 1867.

STANDING COMMITTEE OF THE PARISH FOR 1871.

George Frost.
Charles D. Swain.
N. D. Conant.
J. S. Stanton.
J. A. Brigham.

PASTORAL COMMITTEES FOR 1871.

On the Sick.

Edward T. Danforth.
Alfred Williams.
Mrs. Louise T. Richardson.
Mrs. Caroline A. Newton.
Mrs. Laura Jackson.

APPENDICES.

On Charity.

Andrew W. Newman.
Christopher Tilden.

Mrs. Harriet Winslow.
Mrs. Diana Smith.

On Hospitality.

Gideon Jenkins.
Franklin S. Williams.
L. A. Lauriatt.
John C. Hewes.

T. B. Perkins.
Miss Henrietta Young.
Miss Charlotte Williams.
Miss Lizzie Swain.
J. W. Fillebrown.

On Visitation.

A. J. Patterson.
F. B. Witherell.

Mrs. Catharine Jenkins.
Mrs. Harriet Winslow.
Mrs. Jane L. Patterson.

On Sunday Schools.

Eben. Alexander.
Charles Whittier.

Mrs. Isabell E. Whittier.
Miss Charlotte Williams.
Franklin Williams.

APPENDIX D.

SUNDAY SCHOOL.

Our Memorial would be one-sided and incomplete, were not some special mention made of the Sunday school.

This branch of Christian work was an aftergrowth, an offshoot of the Parish, and from the zeal with which it was received and fostered, we judge that it had small measure of unbelief and doubt with which to contend.

The Sunday school was organized in August, 1836, by the adoption of a Constitution, providing for the annual election by ballot of a Superintendent, Secretary and Treasurer, and Librarian. The growth of the school rendered the office of Assistant Superintendent necessary; and assistants to the Librarian were appointed as needed.

The first Superintendent of the school was Mrs. Dudley Williams, who served two years. She was succeeded by Mrs. Joseph Stratton, who occupied the position four years, a part of the time with the assistance of Mrs. Williams.

In 1837, we find the Rev. Hosea Ballou, 2d, Superintendent, and during that year a meeting was called, and a committee appointed to consider the propriety of introducing singing into the regular exercises. The result of deliberations on the subject was favorable, and singing became a part of the regular service. It was likewise thought best for the teachers to select library books for their pupils, on account of the confusion made by the scholars in selecting their own books, — two very important steps in the line of progress.

Before the close of the year, Mr. Ballou found it necessary to resign his charge, and John Howard was elected to the office.

Up to this time the school had held its sessions only a portion of the year; it was now voted to continue without intermission through the winter, and also to have teachers' meetings once a fortnight.

In June, 1838, the first exhibition was held, greatly to the delight of all who attended.

In 1839, Dudley Williams was elected Superintendent, and a vote was taken that "the teachers be requested to attend their scholars to church after they are dismissed from school." Mr. Williams was annually elected for the period of seventeen years, — a long and honorable service.

In 1847, a Bible Class was formed, and in 1850 the school made its first excursion to Abington.

In 1854, Thaddeus C. Craft, was elected Superintendent, and during that year improvements were made in the vestry. Mr. Craft served three years and was succeeded by Edward Wise, who, in 1861, left the office to the occupancy of Henry B. Metcalf.

Franklin Williams became Superintendent in 1864 and in the summer of 1866 his administration was marked by the enlargement of the vestry to meet the steadily growing wants of the school.

Eben. Alexander succeeded Mr. Williams, but was obliged to resign during his third year of service on account of ill-health. He was followed by W. P. Gannett, who is still Superintendent of the school.

Among the Assistant-Superintendents we find the names of Sarah Turner, Mrs. Stratton, Mrs. Reuben Winslow, Mary Ann Mayo, Mrs. Whitney, John Parker, Mrs. Burrill, Nancy Goody, Christopher Tilden, Frank D. Perkins, William P. Gannett, Charlotte P. Williams.

The Secretaries have been George F. Cook, John D. Young, Alfred Winslow, Joseph Hastings, Joseph C. Howard, Isaac G. Burrill, J. S. Leighton, Joseph Houghton, George F. Davis, William C. Fisk, Frank H. Hastings, T. C. Craft, Edward T. Trafitter, Walter Gill, Wm. H. Jackson.

The Librarians have been John D. Young, Mary H. Smith, John Dove, John Parker, Calvin Young, Joseph Houghton, Franklin Williams, Lafayette Litchfield, Joseph Swain, Henry D. Williams, C. F. Campbell, W. D. Seaver, G. F. Davis, Isaac J. Chubbuck, Sprague Williams, Julius M. Swain, J. G. Hentz, Joseph Houghton, 2d, Warren Anderson, Charles Whittier, Charles F. Kellogg.

The school has had an even prosperity. No great decline, nor spasmodic increase has marred its healthy growth. Harmony has prevailed among its officers, and a good degree of zeal and fidelity has characterized its teachers.

The Bible Class, which was formed in 1847, has been under the care of the several Pastors of the Church, also gentlemen Wm. B. Fowle and Edward Wise. At present it is very ably conducted by Samuel Tucker Cobb. The room, constructed for its accommodation in 1866, is well filled, and much interest is manifested in the lessons.

From this class members are, from time to time, added to the corps of teachers and board of officers; and from the school, as a whole, the Church receives much encouragement and help. The parish fosters the Sunday school, and the school sends its hopeful young life into the Church as a vivifying power, and all are benefited by this mutual service.

SUNDAY SCHOOL TEACHERS, 1871.

Alfred Williams.
Geo. F. Davis.
Edward H. Eaton.
J. Newton Warren.
F. B. Witherell.
Atwell Richardson.
Wm. N. Reed.
Louis A. Lauriatt.
C. Tilden, Jr.
Geo. Craft.
Cha's G. Bird.
Warren L. Anderson.
C. F. Kellogg.
Rev. A. J. Patterson.
F. B. Perkins.
W. P. Gannett.
H. C. Hill.
Walter J. Gill.
Warren Newell.
E. T. Glover.
Wm. Jackson.
James G. Woodman.
Franklin S. Williams.
H. C. Prentis.
Eben Alexander.
H. E. Hunneman.
Cha's Whittier.
Wm. Curtis.
J. W. Fillebrown.
Franklin Williams.
Herbert Barton.
Wm. H. Miner.
Geo. W. Morse.

Ella G. Pike.
Ella Clark.
Lucy M. Williams.
Mrs. M. E. Perry.
   " S. S. Gay.

Emma L. Colligan.
Addie Beal.
Mrs. H. M. Williams.
   " J. N. Warren.
Miss M. L. Swain.
   " H. M. Allen.
   " Millie Rumrill.
   " P. M. Bixby.
Mrs. W. E. Smith.
Miss M. Ella Curtis.
   " A. E. Spencer.
Mrs. Louis A. Lauriatt.
   " Wm. Barton.
Miss Lizzie Kenniston.
   " M. Whiting.
   " H. M. Campbell.
   " Carrie P. Allen.
   " S. Fannie Perry.
Mrs. Isaac Newton.
Miss Addie L. Reed.
   " E. T. Pierce.
   " Abbie S. Oliver.
   " Elsie J. Craft.
   " A. N. Craft.
   " Mary J. Newman.
   " Hattie E. Colligan.
Mrs. H. S. Alexander.
   " H. M. Bacon.
Miss M. J. Richards.
Mrs. Mary Williams.
   " C. H. Call.
Miss H. F. Witherell.
   " Nellie W. Dove.
Mrs. L. F. Richardson.
   " H. C. Hunneman.
   " A. J. Patterson.
Miss Charlotte Williams.
Mrs. F. B. Perkins.
   " J. S. Maffett.

Mrs. E. Bradshaw.
Miss Annie Arnold.
" Ella M. Field.
" Mary F. Woodman.
Mrs. E. J. Whittaker.
" D. E. Whittemore.
" M. M. Clark.
" E. M. Woodward.

ORGANIST.
Eugene L. Buffinton.

CHOIR.
George H. Nason.
Mrs. George H. Nason.
George W. Gardiner.
Mrs. Nellie M. Alden.

APPENDIX E.

As indicative of the fraternal spirit existing among the neighboring churches, we insert the following letters: —

ROXBURY, Jan. 2, 1871.

REV. A. J. PATTERSON: — Seeing in some paper lately that your Church was to have a semi-centennial celebration, I thought to myself that was a meeting I should like to attend and make some remarks, if I might do so with propriety.

Your kind invitation, just received, settles the question of propriety. I have engagements for the whole of Wednesday, but shall make a point of attending your meeting (though it may be at a later hour than I could wish) and say a word or two, if there is time and opportunity.

Cordially yours,
GEORGE PUTNAM,
Pastor of the First Parish Church.

BOSTON HIGHLANDS, Jan. 3, 1871.

REV. A. J. PATTERSON: *Dear Sir*, — I thank you very much for your kind invitation to be present at the semi-centennial services at your Church to-morrow. I am confident the occasion will be one of great interest and joy to you, as you review the successful labors of fifty years, and call to mind the dealings of God with your people.

An early engagement for the evening will prevent me from being with you at the collation. I hope, however, to be able to listen to your Historical Address.

Very truly yours,
HENRY M. KING,
Pastor Baptist Church.

WEDNESDAY, Jan. 4, 1871.

MY DEAR FRIEND: — I have promised myself much pleasure from your jubilee. But the critical illness of my brother, with whom I spend every moment possible, prevents my joining you. I dare not hope that he will live many days.

Accept my congratulations on the prosperity of your Church, and my hopes for its happy centennial.
Always truly yours,
EDW. E. HALE,
Pastor Union Park Street Unitarian Church.

DORCHESTER, Jan. 3, 1871.

DEAR MR. PATTERSON: — You were very kind to think of me in connection with your anniversary to-morrow, and to invite me to be present. It would give me great pleasure to be with you. I wish I could be. But I have been suffering, for a week past, with a severe cold, confining me to the house; and it is still with me to an uncomfortable and disabling extent, and I feel quite sure that it would be an unjustifiable imprudence in me — though I very reluctantly conclude so — to accept your very friendly invitation.

Please accept, for yourself and people, my hearty congratulations upon the occasion, and all the pleasant memories and associations connected with it; on the great prosperity of your society in the present, and its bright prospects for the future. And believe me, yours, fraternally,
NATH'L HALL,
Pastor First Parish Church, Dorchester.

VINE STREET CHURCH, Jan. 3, 1871.

Many thanks, my dear Mr. Patterson, for your most cordial invitation to your Church semi-centennial. May the Lord bless the celebration with the outpouring of his Holy Spirit upon you and your people! We are having meetings this week of prayer, which render it impossible for me to avail myself of the cards you have so kindly sent me.

Respectfully and very truly yours,
JOHN O. MEANS,
Pastor Vine Street Congregational Church.

BOSTON HIGHLANDS, Jan. 5, 1871.

REV. MR. PATTERSON: *Dear Brother*, — I received your kind favor of yesterday, in season to be present with Mrs. Silver at the afternoon celebration, and regretted extremely that an important committee meeting, in Boston, at seven and a half o'clock, required my presence and deprived me the pleasure of being with you in the evening after the collation.

I enjoyed the history of your society intensely, and could not but wish that every member of our own little society could have heard it, and been stimulated by its spirit to persevere. Your society has my warmest congratulation for its success, and ardent prayers for its perseverance in the glorious cause of human salvation by breaking off from sin, by righteousness, and thus coming into the sanctuary of the one great church of God, which consists of all, of whatever name, or sect, or people, who love God and the neighbor.

Very respectfully and truly yours,
ABIEL SILVER,
Pastor Swedenborgian Church.

ADDENDA AND ERRATA.

TREASURERS OF THE PARISH.

Samuel Parker,	1820 to 1832.	Henry S. Ward,	1840 to 1841.
Isaac Gale,	1832 to 1833.	Joseph W. Dudley,	1841 to 1868.
Chester Guild,	1833 to 1838.	Eben. Alexander,	1868 to 1870.
Tilson Williams,	1838 to 1840.	Thad. C. Craft,	1870 to 1871.

Joseph Houghton, 1871.

The Sunday School was organized in 1830. Charles Whittier was never Librarian, but he served faithfully as Vice-Superintendent; and Charles Dove was a careful and efficient Librarian for a number of years. John Colligan is our Sexton, and to his diligent watchful care, we are especially indebted for much of the order and comfort of our Sabbath Home.

Josiah Bugbee,	page 101,	should be	Joseph Bugbee.
T. B. Perkins,	" 102.	" "	Francis B. Perkins.
Christopher Tilden,	" 104,	" "	Christopher Tilden, Jr.
Frank D. Perkins,	" "	" "	Francis B. Perkins.
Edward T. Trafitter,	" "	" "	Edward T. Trofitter.
Isaac G. Burrill,	" "	" "	Isaac S. Burrill.
Isaac J. Chubbuck,	" "	" "	Isaac Y. Chubbuck.
H. C. Prentis,	" 105,	" "	H. C. Prentice.
Mrs. M. E. Perry,	" "	" "	Mrs. M. E. Berry.
Mrs. Mary Williams,	" "	" "	Miss Mary Williams.
Mrs. J. S. Maffett,	" "	" "	Mrs. J. S. Maffitt.
Miss Millie Rumrill,	" "	" "	Miss Nellie Rumrill.
Miss Mary F. Woodman,	" 106,	" "	Miss Mary V. Woodman.

www.ingramcontent.com/pod-product-compliance
Lightning Source LLC
Chambersburg PA
CBHW020129170426
43199CB00010B/701